d
c
1,

Let's Teach Music

IN THE ELEMENTARY SCHOOL

MAURINE TIMMERMAN

Let's Make Music

(Correlated Experiences for the Classroom Teacher)
is published separately

SUMMY-BIRCHARD PUBLISHING COMPANY

EVANSTON, ILLINOIS

Acknowledgments

The author wishes to express her deep appreciation to the following:

For consultant services — Florence Bassett, Spokane City Schools, and Cora Mae Chesnut, Gonzaga University, Bodily Response; The Children's Music Center, 2858 W. Pico Blvd., Los Angeles, Bibliography; William Hartshorn, Supervisor of Music, Los Angeles City Schools, and Dr. Hugh Mullins, Assoc. Prof. Music, Los Angeles State College, Listening; Dr. Archie N. Jones, Prof. Music, University of Texas, Philosophy; and Dr. Louis P. Thorpe, Prof. Psychology, University of Southern California, Psychology.

For manuscript reading — Francis H. Baxter, Assoc. Prof. Music, and Celeste Griffith, Prof. Music, Los Angeles State College.

Thanks are also extended to E. P. Dutton & Co., Inc., for permission to quote (on page 15) three lines from *When We Were Very Young*, by A. A. Milne. New York: E. P. Dutton & Co., Inc., 1924.

Sumco 5152

Foreword

To you who will teach music to children:

You are, no doubt, wondering if you *can* teach, or *how* you can teach. Perhaps you have watched master teachers in action. If not, you will. Some of these teachers you will admire and wish to emulate. Others, you may feel, are wasting time. Perhaps you are seeking a *pattern*. This is not a pattern book. It is a compilation of ideas which were successful in their particular situations.

Many different types of teachers are described here, yet all were effective. You may be vivacious; you may be dramatic; you may be clever; you may be quiet. It does not matter as long as you are sincere. Children are quick to sense sincerity, and they are equally sensitive to insincerity. Do not try to imitate. Be yourself — but take time to evaluate and to improve yourself constantly.

All of the teachers represented here had some characteristics in common. Each one was truly interested in *children,* and each one wanted to contribute toward their musical development. Each one honestly felt that music had something important to give to children — something that could be derived from *no other source,* and without which no life could be complete.

Music makes the listener a different person emotionally, spiritually, and even *physically.* Did you know that there is substantial evidence[*] that music actually changes your breathing, your pulse rate, your blood pressure, and your galvanic skin response? Are you aware that music alleviates fatigue? Have you stopped to think of the effect of music on mood? Do these questions stimulate your thinking regarding the implications for the use of music in the classroom? You who worry about discipline — what do these facts mean to you? What was wrong with the talented young teacher who claimed that her class was so difficult to manage that she dared not attempt to give it musical experiences? She was missing

---

[*]Lundin, Robert William, *An Objective Psychology of Music.* New York: Ronald Press Co., 1953, pp. 132-154.

one possible solution to her problem because she had forgotten the *power* of music.

Music can soothe, and it can excite. It can relax, it can release tension, and it can be a means of "letting off steam." It can afford opportunities for self-expression and for working together. It can build group morale. It can cross the lines of race, color, creed, or social class. It can lift to spiritual heights. All these things it can do so subtly that it does not of itself cause more tensions. It can speak where words fail.

No one can tell you how to teach. If you use the ideas related here it will be necessary for you to adapt them to your children and to your situation. Children like to figure things out for themselves. Do not rob them of the joy of discovery. The teacher who sings a rote song with carefully rehearsed and elaborated gestures may not be as effective as the teacher who sings it simply and who encourages the *children* to interpret it. The teacher who tells in detail the story of program music may not be as successful as the one who piques the curiosity of his pupils and allows them to make up their own stories or to tell their own reactions.

It is much more difficult to guide than to dictate, but guidance pays big dividends. Once an idea is started, it grows like a rolling snowball. As it gathers the contributions (be they ever so small) of each child, it grows, gains momentum, and rolls on to become something bigger than even you or the children had planned. *Give the children a chance!*

Teaching is both a science and an art. It becomes a fine balance between the definite plans and goals of the teacher, the contributions of the pupils, and the beauty of music itself and its effect upon the participants. Some of you may feel handicapped musically, but a good teacher always finds a way.

Maurine Timmerman

Contents

Bibliographies and Additional References will be found at the end of each chapter.

List of Illustrations

vii

Playing, singing, and dancing

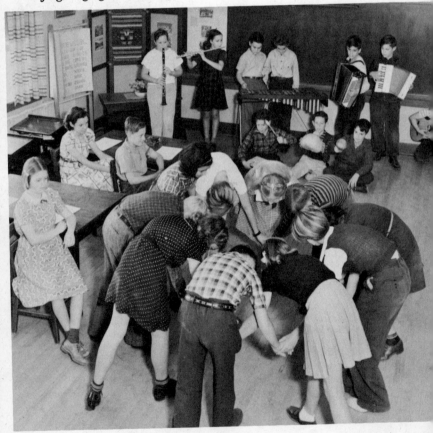

CHAPTER I

Let's See What We Have Done

How many adults hesitate to sing, even in a crowd? Why do they hesitate? Nearly every one who does can trace his insecurity in music to some unhappy experience during childhood.

¶ SOME CASE HISTORIES — The recollections of some of the candidates for the general elementary teaching credential may give us some clues. What happened to these people?

Curtis is a very large fellow. One would guess that he grew very rapidly during his teens. He enjoys listening to music and knows the themes of all the operas, the classical symphonies, and many of the modern works, but he has no muscular coordination. How does he know he lacks coordination? Both his father and his mother were professional musicians, but although Curtis took piano lessons he never did learn to play rhythmically. Whenever either parent tried to help him, the hour ended in a quarrel. Now, he says he will not be able even to clap the rhythm of our songs.

John could sing in elementary school, in fact he sometimes sang for programs. But since his voice has changed he has been unable to sing even for his own pleasure!

Nancy remembers a time when she was thrilled to be a member of the elementary school chorus. After one of the programs her mother put her arm around Nancy's shoulders and said to the teacher, "We know Nancy can't sing, but she tries." That remark did something to Nancy. She stopped trying.

Fred attended a little school where they seldom sang. He knows only two or three songs, and his voice is harsh from disuse. There was no special music teacher, and the classroom teacher never taught any music.

[1]

Ernest's father studied to be a concert violinist, but injured his wrist. He bought his son a little violin, and resolved that he should have every advantage. Ernest was excused from elementary school every day during the music period in order that he should hear no wrong notes, but he could practice his violin at home with the help of his father. He never played in the school orchestra because he might make some errors that would go unnoticed. Worse yet, he might hear some notes that were out of tune! Ernest could not play games because he might injure a finger; he was allowed to keep score. Finally Ernest rebelled, broke his violin, and refused ever to play again. He hates music!

Dale had to sit and listen to some "dull old records" when he was in school. He was required to recognize themes, but he simply wanted to enjoy the music, or to sing!

Tom thinks music is a waste of time. He did not particularly dislike music when he was in school, but he did not learn much.

Anne has never forgiven her mother for not allowing her to play the slide trombone when she was in the first grade. Anne did not know that a first grader does not have arms long enough to play the slide trombone.

Jane liked the piano, but she liked to play "by ear." Her mother would not allow that, for then Jane might not learn to play "the notes." Now Jane feels that she has missed something. She has!

Jean enjoyed singing in school until the boy behind her whispered, "You can't sing!" About the time she was recovering from that blow, the class started to learn the syllables. She never did like those syllables!

Ardith says she is "tone deaf." When asked how she knows, she replies that in school she was placed in the front row with the "sparrows" or monotones. The teacher worked hard with her and urged her to work hard so that she could move back to the "robins" or the "canaries," but the harder she tried, the harder it was to sing. She always choked up and finally she stopped trying. Because she could not sing, and there were no other musical activities, the music period was embarrassing to her.

The above cases represent a sorry picture. Fortunately not all of the recollections are bad.

Alice enjoyed her music in school. She especially enjoyed the rhythmic activities. Don liked playing in the rhythm band, and Arthur liked to listen to records. Mary always enjoyed the days the class created their own songs. Patricia liked singing a part in a chorus. Victor liked everything about his music in the fourth grade because the teacher wore pretty clothes, smiled a lot, and made music a happy time.

What is the difference between the two groups?

Curtis was the victim of talented parents who were impatient and did not understand a growing boy. John's teacher probably did not understand the changing voice. Nancy's feelings were hurt. Fred lacked experience with music. Ernest's father made music lonely drudgery. Dale's school music was not varied or interesting. Tom was not challenged. Anne's mother could have prevented years of resentment by a little timely reasoning, and perhaps the substitution of an instrument Anne could play. Or perhaps Anne's teacher could have helped explain the physical requirements for playing the trombone. Jane's mother was not appreciative of her daughter's creative ability. If the teacher had discovered the *reason* for Jean's withdrawal, had changed her seat, and given a little timely praise, Jean would have been spared some disappointment.

Ardith apparently had a conscientious teacher who did not understand children. If Ardith had not been painfully embarrassed and had experienced some other musical activities in which she was successful, she might have learned to sing.

Group II fared better. Each found a medium of expression through singing, listening, rhythmic or creative activities or through the use of instruments. Each *was successful* in some way. Teachers can take their cues from this group. Of course teachers are not responsible for the errors of parents, but they can make children happier in their school music. In some cases they can even reach the parents.

The attitudes of the students mentioned in this chapter are largely the result of the music education in our schools. Lowell Mason introduced the study of music into the schools as an enjoyable singing experience, but soon came the era when music had to be justified. Teachers began talking about "mental discipline." They stressed note reading and drill. Music lost a great deal of its appeal as an art; it became a science. The notes were all-important. Note reading would prepare the children for singing in fine choruses in later life. Music as an aesthetic experience was almost forgotten. It was no longer a creative art, but had become a task. Examination of old school music texts reveals that the songs were composed for the express purpose of teaching music reading, not because the composer was bursting with something he must give the world. Folk songs and art songs were seldom used. Music, in many cases, was dead. Children seldom sang their school songs outside the classroom. Little thought was given to interest, to desire, to maturation, to love of beauty, and to a need for expression.

Singing was the only music activity. The child who could not sing was completely out of the picture. Music was for the chosen few. If a child rebelled, he was often obliged to copy music or the words of songs as punishment.

In later years a musical experience other than singing was offered in our schools. Listening was introduced. Music memory contests were held. Children were required to identify themes, name the composers, and even tell the dates of the composers' births and deaths. Many teachers confined their objectives for teaching listening to the memorizing of facts. What the music meant to the child was of little consequence. Crutches such as the learning of silly words to the themes of symphonies were often used. Anything was accepted if the objective, the memorizing of themes and facts, was accomplished. Of course this was another experience which appealed to children who were interested in facts rather than in singing. Doubtless some teachers did give their pupils some beautiful experiences in listening, but the average teacher emphasized facts and memory, and felt satisfied if her pupils rated high in the contests.

The rhythm band was another musical experience added to the primary grades. Here, also, rote memorization was the method. The teacher decided what instrument each child should play and when he should play it. Rhythm band became a drill period. Many children enjoyed the activity, but what about the child who always played sticks although he longed to try the drum just once? What musical development and growth were taking place?

Then came the inevitable reaction. Some educators began to realize what was happening. John Dewey's philosophy was taking hold of the music educators, and they began to think of the child rather than the subject. There was talk about learning through experience.

However, music teachers, like the teachers of other subject matter, misunderstood Dewey, and simply threw out all teaching of pupils. Children did only what they wanted to do. They chose the songs and sang them in any manner that pleased them. Teachers feared that encouragement to sing beautifully or to discriminate would cause the children to hate music. What was supposed to be

College students sing and play.
A college class in
"Music for Children."

joy and freedom, in many cases turned out to be license. Any resemblance to a learning situation was strictly coincidental!

This approach also had its limits. Children like to learn. They like to be challenged and to think. They like beautiful experiences, and beautiful experiences need the guidance of a skillful teacher.

The leveling-off process started. Teachers are now aware that the material must be interesting and meaningful to the learner and suited to his maturation level. They also know that the teacher must cause the child to feel a need to learn. They know that there must be many types of musical experience if every child is to be reached, and that each child must find success in one of these experiences. Success in one activity is the most powerful motivating force for trying another. Teachers must do less teaching and more guiding. In this way children will become discriminating, will grow in creativity, and will find the joy that satisfies.

This musical growth cannot take place in solitude. Music is one of the most social activities known. Schools cannot dismiss music from the curriculum with the thought that parents should give children music privately, outside of school. All the lovely folk songs and work songs sprang from people working or playing together. If the songs are to have meaning, they must be sung in a social setting. Rhythmic response has many more possibilities in groups. Even listening to and creating music, although it can be done in solitude, brings about a feeling of closeness, comradeship and even spiritual unity when experienced with others.

There is much talk today about mental health, emotional and social adjustment, attitudes, healthy curiosity and good thinking. Mental hygienists seem to agree that children have a desire for social approval, for mastery, for new experiences, for security, and for individuality. Music can fulfill all of these desires if the teacher is sympathetic, democratic, patient, willing to explore and experiment, industrious, and willing to prepare himself musically. He, himself, must overcome any inhibitions he may have about his own musical performance in order that he may prevent his students from having them. If he *really* cares about children, he will do just that. If he does not care about children, he is in the wrong profession. No matter how intelligent a man is, he cannot learn to swim by reading a book about it. He might learn the strokes, but to swim he must get in the water!

Questions for Class Discussion

1. Try to recall the music classes when you were attending elementary school.
   A. What experiences appealed to you then, and why do you think they did?
   B. What did not appeal, and why?
   C. Which school music teachers appealed most to you, and why?
   D. Which did not appeal, and why?
2. Talk with some children you know. Find out how they feel about the music in their schools.
3. If you are observing in the schools now, try to analyze what you see.
   A. What do you think is especially good?
   B. What do you think could be improved?
4. Try to formulate some aims and objectives as you see them now. As the course progresses make changes as you see them.

Additional References

Adams, Fay, *Educating America's Children*. New York: Ronald Press, 1946, pp. 399-433.

California School Supervisors Association, *Guiding the Young Child*. Boston: D. C. Heath & Co., 1951.

Flagg, Marion, *Musical Learning*. Boston: C. C. Birchard & Co., 1949, pp. 3-46.

Grant, Parks, *Music for Elementary Teachers*. New York: Appleton-Century-Crofts, Inc., 1951, Ch. II.

Krone, Beatrice Perham, *Music in the New School*. (Revised.) Chicago: Neil A. Kjos Music Co., 1947.

Landeck, Beatrice, *Children and Music*. New York: William Sloane Associates, 1952.

Lee, J. Murray and Lee, Dorris May, *The Child and His Curriculum*. New York: Appleton-Century-Crofts, Inc. (Revised), 1950, pp. 586-643.

McConathy, Osbourne et al, *Music for Early Childhood*. New York: Silver Burdett Co., 1952.

Morgan, Hazel Nohavec, *Music in American Education*. Washington, D.C.: Music Educators National Conference, 1955, Ch. 5-9, 23, 29, 30, and pp. 298-304, 313.

Mursell, James, *Education for Musical Growth*. Boston: Ginn & Co., 1948.

Mursell, James, *Music and the Classroom Teacher*. New York: Silver Burdett Co., 1951.

Myers, Louise Kifer, *Teaching Children Music in the Elementary School*. New York: Prentice-Hall, Inc., 1950, Ch. I, VIII.

Nesbitt, Marion, *A Public School for Tomorrow*. New York: Harper & Bros., 1953.

Pillsbury Foundation Study, *Music of Young Children: II. General Observations*. Santa Barbara, Cal.: Foundation for Advancement of Music Education, 1941.

Ragen, William B., *Modern Elementary Curriculum*. New York: The Dryden Press, Inc., 1953, pp. 444-454.

Sheehy, Emma Dickson, *The Fives and Sixes Go to School*. New York: Henry Holt & Co., Inc., 1954.

Sheehy, Emma Dickson, *There's Music in Children*. (Revised.) New York: Henry Holt & Co., Inc., 1952.

Thorpe, Louis, *Child Psychology and Development*. New York: Ronald Press, 1955 (Revised).

Trow, William Clark, *Educational Psychology*. Boston: Houghton Mifflin Co. 1951, Ch. 15, 16.

Round and round we go!

CHAPTER II

Let's Respond with Our Bodies

Rhythmic activities not only help the child to develop his native creative powers, but they provide opportunity for continuous growth through experience. A child may consciously use rhythm creatively or recreatively. A feeling for rhythm is built up in varied experiences. These experiences provide happy releases from emotional tensions, and outlets for the abundant energy of the young child. Rhythm makes a valuable contribution to the development of muscular coordination, freedom in movement, and poise.

¶ What Can Rhythmic Experiences Do for the Child? — Rhythmic experiences can
1. Give the child a real musical experience in which he can be successful.
2. Offer the child an opportunity to create and to express himself in a natural elemental medium.
3. Help the child coordinate in natural movements.
4. Give the child an opportunity for cooperation with others in a social activity.
5. Develop an awareness of basic rhythms through bodily expression.
6. Expand and extend to lay a foundation for musical development.

¶ A Childhood Interest — Children use rhythmic movement from the time they are babies. The child's pat-a-cake combines rhythmic motion and sound. Very often, when a child finds himself on a hard-surfaced floor he starts moving, slapping his feet vigorously on the floor to hear the rhythmic sound. He enjoys pulling a stick across a picket fence, alternating between fast and slow movements and listening to the sounds. He walks, runs, skips, hops, slides, jumps, leaps. His whole being demands activity and motion, and his body is his medium of expression. He needs an outlet for his energy, and he finds deep satisfaction in rhythmic activity.

The interest in sound and movement is there. All that is needed is guidance into fuller and broader experiences.

One teacher motivates interest in sound by asking the children to close their eyes and listen for as many sounds as they can hear. One day her pupils heard the clock ticking, someone clearing his throat, someone's feet moving, traffic outside, and the scrape of chalk in the next room.

Another teacher takes his class for a walk and asks them to listen for different sounds. During one excursion they heard bird songs, a carpenter driving nails, cars and trucks starting, moving, and stopping, a dog barking, a baby crying, and a lawn mower cutting.

The following records are excellent for motivating interest in sound:

Muffin in the City, Young People's Records.
Muffin in the Country, Young People's Records.
Sounds Around Us, Scott, Foresman & Co.
The film, *Rhythm Is Everywhere*.

Children may be encouraged to listen to sounds outside school, and to report to the class at "sharing time." One little boy reported, "My grandmother has some new teeth and they go click-click-click-click!"

¶ MISCONCEPTIONS REGARDING RHYTHMIC ABILITY — Teachers and parents in the past have played phonograph records and asked the children to "do what the music says." If the child did not keep time with the music, they assumed that the child was weak rhythmically. Recent experiments have shown that everyone has a tempo or speed natural to himself. Although it has not been proved, there is some evidence that this natural speed may be closely correlated with the heartbeat and the breathing of the child. One judged unrhythmical when responding to a recording may walk, run, or skip in perfect rhythm at his own speed.

Beginning Activities

Keeping the foregoing knowledge in mind, why not start with the natural tempo of the child? Many teachers respond, "But I can't play the piano well enough to accompany a child's rhythmic movement," or "There is no piano available for accompanying children." Beginning rhythmic experiences can be accompanied without the use of the piano. It is best to catch a child in his natural tempo at a time when he is unaware of being observed. For example, as a child walks across the room the teacher might say, "This is the way your feet sounded," as she claps the rhythm of his walk. As other children walk back and forth across the room, the teacher claps her hands in time with their feet. After a few trials similar to these, she asks the other children to watch Johnny cross the room, and as he comes back to make their hands say "what Johnny's feet say." Johnny is moving at his own pace, and the children are both *hearing* and *seeing* his rhythm. Initial experiences should involve the *large* muscles or the body as a *whole*.

Variations may be introduced in numerous ways. "Tom, suppose you have played ball until you are very tired. Show us how you would walk home." Or "Mary, today is your birthday. Suppose you know, when you get home, you will find something you have been wanting for a long time. Show us how you would go home." This would lead to either a fast walk or a run. "Show us how many ways you can walk," also brings forth variations such as walking forward, backward, sideways, on tiptoe, on heels, crossing the feet, on the sides of the feet, lifting feet high, dragging the feet, crouching, long steps, and short steps.

There are three kinds of rhythmic activities, namely:

1. Free creative bodily movements.
2. Impersonation or dramatization.
3. Use of the fundamental rhythms such as walking, running and skipping.

¶ FREE BODILY MOVEMENTS — When children are able to follow the beat of music, an entire new world is opened to them. They should be given ample opportunity to discover this world for themselves. Encouragement from the teacher will help the children find many exciting and satisfying experiences. "Tom has found a gallop!" "Let's watch Judy whirl!" "O! Did you see Pat leap?" and "Let's see how high you can lift your knees, Jennifer!" will bring eager responses from the children. Music for this sort of activity should be rhythmically strong. The Ethnic Folkways records are excellent for this type of action. Mrs. Gertrude Knight shows this approach in her film, *Building Children's Personalities with Creative Dancing*.

Impersonation and dramatization will be discussed in the chapter on creative activities.

¶ RECOGNITION OF THE FUNDAMENTAL RHYTHMIC MOVEMENTS — After varied experiences in walking, running, and skipping at their own tempos, the children should be able to recognize these rhythms when they are played on rhythm instruments. These are the *primary* rhythms. Some children can be introduced to line notation at this point. (Use the flat side of a small piece of chalk for this, or use a flannel board.)

Walking — — — —
Running - - - - - - -
Skipping — - — - — - — -

Children can devise games using rhythmic activities. One child could point to the line notation for walking, running or skipping, and ask another to respond. One child could move rhythmically and ask another to draw or to point to the corresponding line notation.

¶ RECOGNITION OF RHYTHM IN NAMES — Children enjoy discovering the rhythm of their own names. A child announces his name and the class claps, steps, draws, or plays the rhythmic pattern on a rhythm instrument. Examples: John Dawes — —, Mar-y Burn-ey - - - -, Mar-i-lyn John-son - - - — -.

¶ USE OF SPACE — The new kindergarten rooms are planned to provide for activity. In some cases a period in the gymnasium, the auditorium, or the cafeteria is desirable to permit freer movement and more satisfying experiences. Little children can learn to run, skip, gallop, and leap together without bumping and jostling.

Strict organization is neither necessary nor desirable, but consciousness of space and respect for individuals are. If the space permits, the children may simply scatter and move in the same general direction. Children can move freely even within groups.

¶ VARIED SPACE PATTERNS — A circle formation is good, but there are other possible patterns. Children may move diagonally from corner to corner, forward and backward, and from side to side of a given space. Spirals, serpentines, and follow-the-leader offer

Children clap to music

Creative rhythms to ethnic music

opportunities. It is well to use formations other than the circle, and encourage originality, since imitation naturally follows when the children are moving in a line. Children may suggest shapes and patterns they would like to try.

¶ BASIC MOVEMENTS — There are many types of movement (including the primary rhythms) which may be classified thus:

1. Movements from place to place (locomotion)
   Even rhythms

Walk	Hop	Leap
Run	Jump	

   Uneven rhythms

Skip	Gallop	Slide

2. Movements in place (axial motion)

Swinging	Swaying
Rocking	Bending-lifting
Pulling-pushing	Rising-falling
Twisting-turning	Shaking-beating
Reaching-stretching	

¶ CREATIVE FOOT PATTERNS — Children can learn to combine the fundamental rhythms. Example: Run run run jump! Run run run jump! If encouraged, little children are very creative. They will create countless interesting patterns which adults, with all their years of inhibitions, could never imagine. Children should be allowed many opportunities to try their creative powers. Asking them to put a "surprise" at the beginning, the end, or in the middle encourages variety. The "surprise" above was the jump. Children use whirls, leaps, somersaults, bows, and many other activities.

Accompaniment for Rhythmic Activities

Accompaniment for the initial rhythmic activities should *follow* rather than dominate the movement.

Suggested accompaniments include:

1. Self-accompaniment
   A. The beat of the movement itself upon the floor.

B. Clapping as pupils move. One group claps as the other group moves.

C. Chanting or word accompaniment. *Examples:*

See me skip and skip and skip.
Run on tiptoe, tiptoe, tiptoe.
Galloping ponies, galloping ponies.

2. Mother Goose rhymes and poetry

If the teacher has these well in mind and can instantly and appropriately use them, they will be a source of enjoyment and awareness for the child. *Examples:*

Jack be nimble, Jack be quick,
Jack jump over the candlestick!

Christopher Robin goes
Hoppity, hoppity,
Hoppity, hoppity, hop.
— A. A. MILNE (17:60)

Once I saw a little bird
Come hop, hop, hop;
So I said, "Little bird,
Will you stop, stop, stop?"
And was going to the window
To say, "How do you do?"
But he shook his little tail,
And away he flew.
— *Traditional Rhyme*

Walter de la Mare and A. A. Milne have written a wealth of material suitable for this type of accompaniment.

3. Song accompaniment

A song, sung by the teacher, appropriate to the child's activity will not only bring pleasure to the child at the moment, but may awaken his rhythmic awareness and interest in music.

Songs may be used as accompaniment for group movement. They may be sung by one group as the other moves, by the group that is moving, or by the teacher while all the children move.

Here are some suitable songs for kindergarten and first grade. (See p. 40, numbered bibliography.)

From *American Folk Songs for Children.* (24) Seeger, Ruth Crawford
    Hey Jim Along, Jim Along Josie   72
    Run, Chillen, Run   92
    All Around the Kitchen   94
    Walk Along, John   142
From *American Singer*, Bk. I, Beattie et al (5)
    My Pony   129
    Old Mister Elephant   80
    Roller Skating   135
    Walking Song   112
From *The First Grade Book,* Pitts et al (19)
    Run and Run   12
    Skipping Song   16
    Galloping   22
    Trotting   23
From *The Kindergarten Book,* Pitts et al (20)
    Running   10
    Skipping Is Fun   13
    We're Galloping   18
    Tippy Tiptoe   20
From *Music Through the Day,* Mursell et al (18)
    Giddy-ap, Pony   104
    Let's Go Walking   49
    Tippy Tippy Tiptoe   10
    Toodala   13
From *Music 'round the Clock,* Krone et al (11)
    Busy Workers   17
    Come Out and Play   26
    Fun to Be a Helper   15
    See My Pony   24
From *New Music Horizons*, Bk. I, McConathy et al (12)
    The Candy Shop   30
    The Merry-Go-Round   8
From *Our First Music,* Armitage et al (2)
    Galloping   114

4. Drum accompaniment (see p. 23)

Walk — $\frac{2}{4}$ '$\frac{3}{4}$, or $\frac{4}{4}$ meter, using quarter notes (♩   ♩)

Run — $\frac{2}{4}$, $\frac{3}{4}$, or $\frac{4}{4}$ meter, using eighth notes (♫ ♩ ♫ ♩)

Skip, Gallop, Slide — $\frac{2}{4}$, $\frac{3}{4}$, or $\frac{4}{4}$ meter ♩♪ ♩♪

or fast $\frac{6}{8}$, $\frac{9}{8}$, or $\frac{12}{8}$ ♩ ♪♪ ♩ ♪

Swinging-swaying, Rocking — $\frac{6}{8}$ ♩.   ♩. or ♩ ♪♪ ♩ ♪

or $\frac{3}{4}$ ♩   ♩

Jumping — $\frac{2}{4}$ ♩   ♩

Leaping — $\frac{2}{4}$ ♩   ♩ or $\frac{6}{8}$ ♩.   ♩.

5. Instrumental accompaniment

Teachers who are at ease in playing the piano (or other instrument) may make interesting accompaniments to the rhythmic activities of the children. They must remember to *follow* the children during the initial stages.

Further Beginning Activities

¶ FOLLOWING THE RHYTHM OF THE DRUM AND OTHER INSTRUMENTS — After children have had sufficient opportunities for activity at their own speed, they are ready to follow a given tempo. Running, walking, or skipping rhythms can be played on the drum or other rhythm instruments, on the autoharp, the piano or other instrument, or on the phonograph. The children can fit their activity to the music that is played. These rhythmic patterns should be played one at a time at first. After some experience with each type separately the children are ready to combine rhythms. The teacher should give no warning when the change is to come, but should move without pause from one rhythm to another. Children should have the joy of discovery as much as possible. The activity should be kept in the spirit of a game rather than a drill.

Many games can be built on rhythmic activities. In "Copycat" or "Ditto" one player taps, steps, or plays a rhythmic pattern on a rhythm instrument. He then selects another player to imitate the pattern. If the second player is successful he may be "it" and choose someone to copy his pattern, and so on.

Watch me!

Leaping

Following the drum

¶ RESPONSE TO LONG NOTES — *Twinkle, Twinkle Little Star* is a good song for this activity. The children listen and respond to the music by walking or clapping the rhythm pattern of the melody. They discover the long notes on "star," "are," "high" and "sky," and indicate them by slow steps or holds. There are many ways in which children can be led to discover that these are two-beat notes. While one group steps, the remainder of the class might clap the underlying pulse and find that they clap twice during the slow steps. The moving group should be encouraged to show the extra beat in some way other than stepping. They will think of such things as step-bend, step-clap, and step-bow. Songs with three-beat notes and songs with four-beat notes follow.

Teachers who play the piano will find the Hood and Schultz technique interesting (10:59 — p. 59, book #10; see page 40).

¶ RESPONSE TO THE RHYTHMIC PATTERN OF THE MELODY — The *rhythmic pattern of the melody* follows the melody of an instrumental composition. In a song it usually follows the words exactly; i.e., a long note occurs with a corresponding long word. Children in the kindergarten and the first grade should be able to clap this rhythm. Games may be played wherein the teacher or a child with a good sense of rhythm claps the rhythmic pattern of the melody of a song and the rest of the class identifies the song. One class devised a game, "Stop the Music." The child who was "it" clapped the rhythmic pattern of a familiar song until a member of the class raised his hand. If the latter identified the song correctly, the whole class sang the song, and the "namer" became "it."

¶ RESPONSE TO THE UNDERLYING BEAT OR PULSE — The *underlying beat* is the steady underlying pulse that continues, regardless of the tune. All of the beats are of the same length. In $\frac{2}{4}$ meter the beats would be expressed by quarter notes throughout the song ♩   ♩ . In $\frac{3}{8}$ meter the notes would be expressed by eighth notes throughout the song ♪ ♪ ♪ , or until a meter change. Any child who can follow the drum or the piano can learn to clap or step the underlying pulse as well as the rhythmic pattern of the melody. After experience in clapping or stepping these two rhythms separately, the class may be divided, one half clapping the underlying pulse, and the other half, the rhythmic pattern of the melody. The children can suggest different methods of clapping each. For example, one class divided in half, and those clapping the underlying pulse patted their laps; the other group clapped their hands. This activity made a distinction in sound between the two rhythms. Later the same class suggested that some children could step each part while the others clapped the two rhythms.

¶ RESPONSE TO THE STRONG BEAT OR ACCENT — Teachers may introduce the accent by singing songs, accenting the first beat of the measure; by playing the piano (or other instrument); or by use of records. It is better that the *teacher*, rather than the children, sings the song, to allow the children to hear the strong beat. Children may step or clap the underlying pulse and discover that some beats are stronger than others. They may be encouraged to show the strong beats by stepping or clapping *only* the *strong* beats. They will suggest other ways of showing the weak beats. One class clapped the strong beats and waved their hands on the weak beats. Another stepped the strong beats and pointed their toes on the weak beats. However, they should decide on some activity different from the ones selected for showing long notes. If they count ONE on each accent, adding counts for the number of beats between the accents, they will discover that some music swings in 2's, some in 3's, and some in 4's. Sometimes it helps if the class says "Strong, weak," or "Strong, weak, weak," or "Strong, weak, weak, weak," as the case may be. Music with definite accents should be used for the initial efforts in this activity. Fast waltzes should be avoided, because they are usually felt one beat to the measure. Ability to distinguish between music swinging in 2's and music swinging in 4's is not too important for the young child. Many adults find this difficult. As the teacher plays the music, she can heavily accent the first beat of the measure and play the other three beats lightly, but most recordings have a slight secondary accent on the third beat of music swinging in 4's. This secondary accent may confuse the children.

Children like to use their imaginations in bodily activities. They like to throw, kick, bounce and bat balls, jump ropes, row boats, chop wood, shovel, swim, skate, and do all kinds of activities to music. The strong beat can be felt in many activities. One ingenious teacher made the old folk song, "Shuckin' of the Corn" (25:13) very real to a class of elementary school children. The boys and girls vigorously pulled the husks loose on one strong beat and tossed them over their shoulders on the following one, continuing throughout the song, singing as they shucked.

In former years, workers created songs to furnish a rhythmic beat to follow as they worked. Sea chanteys, miners' songs, lumber-jack songs, and even cowboy songs are examples of work songs. The sailors in olden times needed to work together rhythmically to man the capstan and pull up the anchor, to hoist the sails, and to pump the water out of the hold. A lead singer, the chanteyman, was hired to sing the verses and set the tempo, and the other sailors joined in on the choruses as they worked. As many verses were sung as were needed to accomplish the task. If a song were too short, the chantey-man made up more verses on the spot. Usually, the songs were meant to amuse the workers as well as to furnish the rhythm.

Children can be encouraged to show the swing of the music on the chalkboard, making designs such as

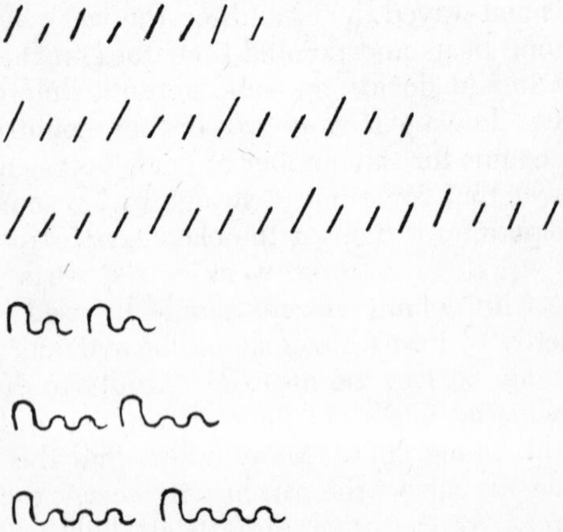

/ / / / / / /

/ / / / / / / / / /

/ / / / / / / / / / / / / / /

∿ ∿

∿ ∿

∿ ∿

Such patterns make excellent bases for art work in border designs and finger-painting. Some admirable examples of this sort of design may be found in *We Sing* (4). One class made borders for the music bulletin board. Another made designs to decorate the kegs and buckets from which their drums were made.

✓Finding the accent leads easily to conducting. Students usually bring the right arm *down* on the ONES or accents. Most students naturally bring their arms *up* on the second beat. They generally make triangles for the music swinging in 3's. After some experimen-tation it is well to show the older children traditional conductor's beats. Intermediate and upper grade children enjoy conducting.

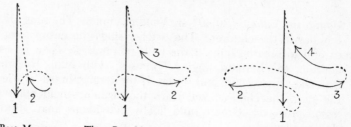

Two-Beat Measure   Three-Beat Measure   Four-Beat Measure

They should be given many opportunities to conduct their class-mates in singing. This activity will be useful to many students throughout their lives. Informal gatherings often need song leaders.

After the students are experienced in discovering the accents in music that keeps the same beat pattern throughout, it is good to play music changing from 2's to 3's to 4's, varying the sequence from time to time. No warning should be given of the coming change; the children should be allowed to discover the changes themselves. This activity may be used with the drum, the autoharp, or other instruments if there is no piano available.

¶ COMBINING THE ACCENT, THE UNDERLYING PULSE, AND THE RHYTHMIC PATTERN OF THE MELODY — The class may be divided, one half clapping the underlying pulse and the other the accents. The rhythmic pattern of the melody and the accents can also be combined. After experience of this type the class may be divided into thirds, one third clapping the accents, one the underlying pulse and one the rhythmic pattern of the melody. Children should be encouraged to think of different sound effects for each part. They can also step the various combinations. Finally they can combine all three activities, with part of the students clapping and some of them stepping. They feel that this is a major accomplishment.

¶ DISCOVERING PHRASES — A phrase is a musical thought, and it may be indicated by a slight pause, a long note, a rest, or by a breath mark at the end. Breath marks are large commas placed above the music. Occasionally a long curve is placed above the music included in a phrase. In a well-written song, the word phrases and the musical phrases correspond.

Songs with definite phrases should be used when introducing this activity. *Go in and out the Windows* (13:27) or *Round and*

Round the Village (20:40) are good examples. The song should be familiar to the children. The teacher sings the entire song, being careful to breathe only at the ends of phrases. Then he asks the children to alternate singing "phrases" with him. He sings the first, they the second, and so on. If the term "phrase" is used from the start, the children will learn the meaning incidentally as the lesson proceeds. Groups, and finally individuals, may alternate in singing phrases.

This may be followed by the teacher singing an *unfamiliar* song that contains definite phrase endings. This time the pupils close their eyes and indicate the phrases with their arms. Each motion of the arms should start simultaneously with the phrase and continue until it ends. Children will think of many ways to show phrases. Closing their eyes encourages children to think for themselves, rather than to imitate others.

One arm may also be used to indicate phrases by drawing arcs in the air. One or two children may draw the arcs on the board as the teacher and the other pupils sing. These arcs may then be numbered.

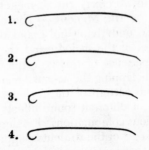

Some examples of songs with definite phrases are:

From *American Singer*, Bk. II, Beattie, et al (6)
    The Cowboy   p. 62
From *Merry Music*, Armitage, et al (1)
    The Pretender   61
From *Music 'round the Clock*, Krone, et al (11)
    God Loves Me   70
From *New Music Horizons*, Bk. II, McConathy, et al (13)
    Oh Where Has My Little Dog Gone?   20

From *Singing and Rhyming*, Pitts, et al (22)
    Six Little Dogs   33

Suitable recordings with definite phrases may be used in a similar manner. "Walk with Direction Change" from *Rhythmic Activities* by Florence Bassett and Cora Mae Chesnut is excellent. The R. C. A. Victor *Elementary School Record Library* has many records suitable for phrase recognition. This is an activity which should be continued throughout the elementary school and into junior and senior high school. Children should be conscious of phrases both in singing and in playing instruments. As the child becomes more experienced, music with less obvious phrases may be used. Children will not always agree on phrase endings. Neither do musicians!

Pupils may step the rhythmic pattern of the melodies of songs, instrumental music or recordings, indicating the ends of phrases. Originality should be encouraged. Some possibilities include change of direction, bows, curtseys, and whirls. Colored scarves may be used effectively, a different color for each phrase. Rhythm instruments may also be used. (See p. 46.)

Dance rhythms

¶ RECOGNITION OF LIKE AND UNLIKE PHRASES — Suppose the
preceding or a similar technique has been used with the song, *Oh
Where Has My Little Dog Gone?* (13:20). The arcs have been
drawn on the board. Some teachers proceed by singing the first
phrase and labelling it "A." The children are instructed to listen for
any other "A's" as the teacher sings the entire song with "loo" or
other neutral syllable. They will discover that the third phrase is
also "A." Since the second phrase was different, it may be called
"B." As they listen to the song again, the children will undoubtedly
disagree about the melody of the fourth phrase. Some will think
it is like the second, and others will insist that it is different. The
teacher can moderate the discussion and lead the children to agree
that the two phrases are *similar,* but not exactly the same. The
children may devise a way to show the similarity. A chart may be
made on the chalkboard such as:

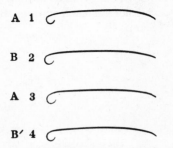

Other teachers vary the procedure from the point where each
group sings a phrase. The teacher sings the first phrase with "loo"
and asks, "Whose phrase did I sing?" Both groups 1 and 3 claim
the phrase. When both groups sing the words of their phrases, the
class discovers that the musical phrases are identical. In the same
manner they find that the second and fourth phrases are similar but
not identical.

Children may use like, similar, and different bodily expression,
or colored scarves or pompons to show their discoveries. They may
create their own dances using suitable songs or recordings. Often
the words of a song will suggest the rhythmic interpretation. For
the use of instruments with phrases see p. 47.

Beginning Rhythmic Notation

¶ LINE RHYTHMIC NOTATION — Children have previously "pictured" walking, running and skipping music (see p. 12). When they have enough muscular coordination to handle chalk easily, they can write the *line rhythmic notation* ("picture") of the primary rhythms as they are actually being played on rhythm instruments, the piano, or the phonograph.

This activity leads easily into line rhythmic notation for the rhythmic patterns of the melodies of simple familiar songs.

Example 1   Example 2

— — —   —   —   ———
Hot cross buns,

— — —   —   —   ———
Hot cross buns,

¯ ¯ ¯ ¯ ¯ ¯   — — — — — — —
One a pen-ny, two a pen-ny,

— — ———   —   —   ———
Hot cross buns.

Some children find it easier to place the notation directly above the words (Example 1); others prefer to do it without the words (Example 2). Children will find that there are actually only two different phrases in this song. The first, second and fourth phrases are identical.

It is not necessary always to use a whole song for this activity. Writing the line notation for one or two phrases of a song will often suffice.

Some teachers introduce the measure bars at this time. Others present the notes first. If the bars are introduced at this point, the children can locate the accents in some simple song such as *Hot Cross Buns*. Then they suggest ways of showing them on line notation. The teacher should guide them to the use of vertical lines *before* each strong beat in order that the singers will be ready to sing the strong beats. The use of vertical lines prevents confusion with the horizontal lines of line notation. With the bars added, the music will look like this:

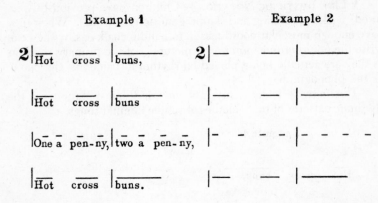

Example 1   Example 2

Because the song swings in twos, the 2 should be placed before the song.

¶ CONVERTING TO STANDARD MUSICAL NOTATION — One teacher played walking music and asked a child to write it on the board in line notation. He followed the same procedure with running music. (See Example 1.)

Example 1   Example 2

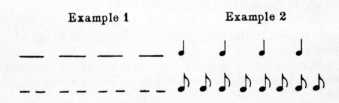

Then he appealed to children's love of the dramatic by saying he would perform a magic trick and change the line notation into real musical notes! (Example 2.) Using the flat side of a short piece of chalk, he rounded the note heads, then added stems and flags. A child who had been taking music lessons named the notes "quarter notes" and "eighth notes." The class decided from then on to use the real names. The teacher then showed the children a chart like this:

The class discussed the difference between the quarter and the eighth notes. One small boy observed that the fast ones had "wings." The teacher explained that eighth notes could be separate or joined together.

The class made a game. One player pointed to the notes and his partner played them on the drum. If the partner played correctly, he was permitted to choose another partner to play the drum while he pointed, and so on. Then they reversed the process and the pointer was required to point to the kind of music the drummer played.

A few days later this same teacher placed on the board the chart the class had made for *Hot Cross Buns*. The children were asked to change the line notation to notes. Most of them could manage the quarter and the eighth notes, but a little guidance was required for making the long notes. A child who was taking private lessons showed the class how to make half notes, and the chart was completed:

The class then added half notes to their games.

It was easy to change running notes (eighths) to skipping by adding a dot to each long eighth and a second "wing" to the short ones. The latter were named "sixteenth notes" and added to the charts and games ♩. ♪ ♩. ♪ ♩. ♪ ♩. ♪ . It was a natural conclusion that the dot lengthened a note. This made the dotted half (♩.) easy. Phrases from familiar songs containing the various note values were worked out in line notation and changed to notes. The whole note (o) was introduced when encountered in a song.

Hood and Schultz (10:87) have some interesting ways of introducing notation. The flannel board offers possibilities in note recognition. A teacher should use her ingenuity and try various procedures. What works for one teacher does not necessarily work for another. A good teacher tries various ways, and eventually evolves one of her own to suit her needs and those of her students. Groups differ, and individuals differ.

Using the Music Books

Children will be eager to see how these things they have discovered are used in their music books. Some educators advocate books in the hands of the children from the start. (Some schools cannot afford this.) Others reserve the books until the second or third grade. The children will observe the following:

A. The measure bars

After the children have responded to the accents with their bodies and have marked them with vertical lines on the board, they may open their books and locate them in some familiar song. Doubtless some child will call them "measure bars." This is the time to explain that music, as well as other things, is measured. The room length is measured by foot rulers. Music is measured by measure bars. These bars divide the music into "measures" — the space between two bars. Children will notice that there is a "double bar" at the end of each song (‖), and no bar at the beginning of each "staff" across the page. They can count the measures in a staff and in a song. The teacher may ask the pupils to read the words in a particular measure. This will show that the measure is a means of quickly locating a place in a song.

Further exploration shows that music does not always begin on the first beat of the measure. Often the first word of a song does not fall on the accent.

B. The measure signature

When they sing the song, the children will discover that a song swinging in 2's has 2 for the top number at the beginning of the song. A song swinging in 3's has 3 for the top number, and so on. This leads to the generalization that the top number in the "measure signature" tells how the song swings. One teacher places the word "signature" on the board and covers all but the first four letters. The class discusses the word and the fact that their name signatures are their signs. The numbers at the beginning of a song are the signature for the measure.

If the children are curious about the lower number, they may locate a measure with two (three, or four, as the top number indicates) notes. Suppose they are quarter notes. 4 stands for quarter notes, 8 for eighth notes. In $\frac{2}{4}$ measure the song would swing in 2's and two *quarter notes* (or notes of equal value, such as a quarter and two eighth notes) would be required to fill the measure. The measure signature could have been written ♩. In $\frac{3}{4}$ measure three quarter notes would fill the measure. It could have been written ♩. In $\frac{4}{8}$ measure four eighth notes (or their equivalent) would fill the measure. It could have been written ♪. In $\frac{4}{4}$ measure four quarter notes fill the measure. Sometimes ℂ is used in place of $\frac{4}{4}$.

C. Notes and rests

After children have responded to and recognized notes, they should observe them in their books. A wise teacher will select each song with as few *new* problems as possible. Some songs suitable for introductory work include:

1. Quarter and eighth notes and their rests (♩ 𝄽 and ♪ 𝄾)

From *Music 'round the Clock*, Together We Sing Series (11)
    Tick Tock   7
    See My Pony   24
From *New Music Horizons*, Bk. III (14)
    The Bridge of Avignon   72
    Travel   23
From *Singing and Rhyming*, Our Singing World Series (22)
    Six Little Dogs   33
    Intry Mintry   22

2. Half notes and rests (♩ ▬)

From *American Singer*, Bk. III (7)
    The Cobbler   19
    In France   64
From *Merry Music* (1)
    Good Morning Song   17
    Singing   13
From *Music 'round the Clock* (11)
    'Round the Clock   4
    My Little Cats   34
From *New Music Horizons*, Bk. III (14)
    The Good Shepherd   88
    Sing a Song of Sixpence   45
From *Singing and Rhyming* (22)
    The Tailor and the Mouse   34
    High, Betty Martin   43

3. Dotted half notes (♩.)

From *American Singer*, Bk. III (7)
    Old Pompey   94
    The Bee and the Ant   167
From *Merry Music* (1)
    A Lovely Color   131
    God, Who Made the Earth   47
From *Music 'round the Clock* (11)
    Frisky Wisk   22
    My Bronco   47
From *New Music Horizons*, Bk. III (14)
    Sea Horse   10

4. Whole notes (o)

5. Dotted eighth followed by sixteenth (♪. ♪ or ♪. ♪)

6. Sixteenth notes (♬♬ or ♪ ♪ ♪ ♪)

7. Table of notes and corresponding rests

Teaching the Dotted Quarter Note
Followed by the Eighth (♩. ♪)
(*When the quarter note is the beat note.*)

Children already know that dotted notes are longer. The rhythmic figure (♩. ♪) is found in several familiar songs including *America; America, the Beautiful; Come, Thou Almighty King;* and *All Through the Night.* The class sings one of the above songs (probably *America*), clapping the rhythmic pattern of the melody. The class may then divide into two groups, half clapping the underlying pulse, while the other half claps the rhythmic pattern of the melody. The class may use two different sounds, such as clapping the hands for the rhythmic pattern, and clapping on the lap for the underlying pulse. In this way they discover that the dotted quarter note is held over the second beat, and the eighth note is "slipped in" after the second beat and before the next beat. Some teachers feel that this physical approach is much better at this time than the mathematical approach which is so often used.

Other teachers feel that the above approach is not accurate and prefer to have the pupils tap down and up on each beat. The quarter note is held for two taps and the eighth note is sung on the second upbeat. This method approaches the mathematical method and is more accurate.

Some songs suitable for further application include:

From *American Singer*, Bk. IV (8)

Teaching the Dotted Quarter Note as the Beat Note in $\frac{6}{8}$ $\frac{9}{8}$ or $\frac{12}{8}$

The children should have in their repertoire many rote songs in $\frac{6}{8}$ measure. Galloping, skipping, sailing, swinging songs, and, often, lullabies are written in $\frac{6}{8}$ measure. Children should respond to songs in this rhythm with their bodies *before* they study them on the printed page. *Row, Row, Row Your Boat* is excellent as a pattern song. It is found in *American Singer*, Bk. IV (8:38), *New Music Horizons*, Bk. IV (15:95), and *Singing and Rhyming* (22:105), but it should be sung with the books closed. The pupils sing the song in unison at a rapid tempo, clapping the underlying pulse. They find

American folk dancing

that it swings in 2's, strong-weak. After the song has been sung several times, books should be opened. The students discover that the first measure has two beats and two dotted quarter notes. From these facts they try to create a measure signature. If they remember that $\frac{2}{4}$ could be written $\begin{smallmatrix}2\\ \end{smallmatrix}$, they should evolve $\begin{smallmatrix}2\\ \end{smallmatrix}\cdot$. In the song book, however, the measure signature is $\frac{6}{8}$. If the students try to clap the underlying pulse in 6's as they sing rapidly, they will soon find that fast $\frac{6}{8}$ is easier swinging in 2's. They locate measures containing all eighth notes and find that there are three eighth notes to a beat. They also discover that ♩ ♪ makes one beat, and that ♩. has two beats.

Some teachers use word rhythms such as:

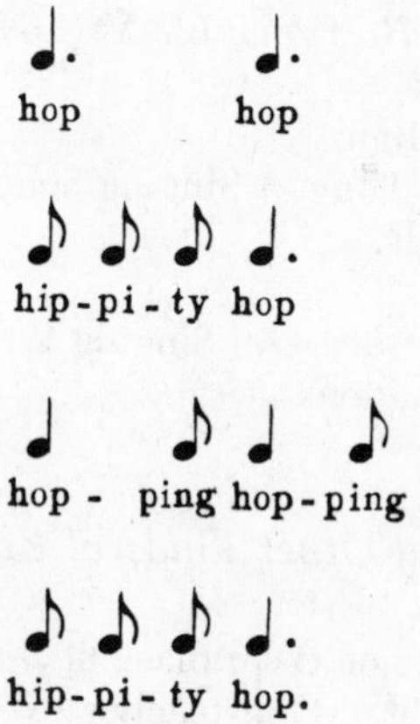

♩.   ♩.
hop   hop

♪ ♪ ♪ ♩.
hip - pi - ty hop

♩   ♪ ♩ ♪
hop - ping hop - ping

♪ ♪ ♪ ♩.
hip - pi - ty hop.

or

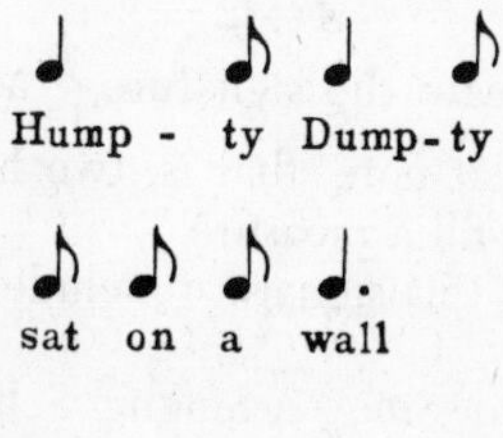

♩   ♪ ♩ ♪
Hump - ty Dump - ty

♪ ♪ ♪ ♩.
sat on a wall

The words may be chanted, clapped, sung or played on rhythm instruments, and the notation observed.

Other suitable familiar songs for fast $\frac{6}{8}$ measure include *Oats,*

Peas, Beans; Pop Goes the Weasel; When Johnny Comes Marching Home. Beautiful Dreamer is written in $\frac{9}{8}$ and swings in 3's. $\frac{12}{8}$ measure generally swings in 4's.

Slow songs in $\frac{6}{8}$ measure may be sung six beats to a measure. *Silent Night* is an example.

If the students write *Row Your Boat* in line notation they will discover that ♩ ♪ ♩ ♪ is — · — · or skipping music. This fact may facilitate reading.

Some suitable songs in $\frac{6}{8}$ measure include:

From *American Singer*, Bk. V (9)

Rowing	p. 100
The Privateer	103

From *New Music Horizons*, Bk. V (16)

The Pigeons	142
The Derby Ram	143

From *Our Land of Song*, A Singing School Series (3)

Roll, My Ball	147
Rio Grande	63

From *Singing Together*, Our Singing World Series (23)

Come Ye Maidens	147
Good-By	146

Teaching Other Kinds of Beat Notes

On page 31 the use of **C** in place of $\frac{4}{4}$ measure was mentioned. Occasionally one sees **¢** . One teacher explains this quickly thus:

$$4 \div 2 = 2$$
$$4 \div 2 = 2$$

The children then create the signature $\frac{2}{2}$ and reason that the half note would be the beat note, that is, two half notes or their value would be required to fill a measure.

Some songs with this signature include:

From *Our Land of Song*, A Singing School Series (3)

When Your Potato's Done	p. 127
Turn, Cinnamon, Turn	134

From *Singing Together*, Our Singing World Series (23)

Harvest Fun	150

Rhythmic activities are necessarily feeling and listening activities. At one time rhythm was considered intellectual and based upon mathematical concepts. This does not mean that thinking is no longer involved in rhythmic activities, but it does mean that feeling and pulse are basic. These concepts must be attained by participation in many rhythmic activities.

It is of the utmost importance that music be kept an aesthetic and beautiful experience. Suppose strong accents are needed for initial activities. Rather than distort a lovely lullaby, the teacher should select vigorous music in which the accents are strong and are an integral part of the music.

Questions for Class Discussion

1. Contrast the grasp of rhythm through bodily movement with an intellectual or mathematical understanding of rhythm. Discuss the advantages and the disadvantages of each.
2. What is the most important point to remember when introducing young children to rhythmic experience?
3. Which child do you consider the more deficient: the one who cannot "keep time," or the one who cannot "carry a tune?" Give reasons for your answers.
4. Read about Jacques Dalcroze and eurythmics. In what ways are eurythmics used in the public schools of today?
5. How can rhythmic activities help in reading music? How might they help in reading words?
6. How can rhythmic activities help in singing?
7. What is meant by free or undirected rhythmic expression? By formal or directed rhythmic activities? Name some of each type.
8. What are the dangers to be avoided in folk dances, singing games, action and motion songs?
9. Of what value is "conducting" to children?

Written Assignment

1. Write *Go Tell Aunt Rhodie* in line rhythmic notation. Indicate accents.
2. Write the following in line rhythmic notation, with accents:

> This proud land across the sea
> Was found by Vikings brave.
> The Pilgrims and the Spaniards came
> Across the ocean wave.
>
> *Margaret MacPherson*, Aged 10

Bibliography

1. Armitage, Theresa et al, *Merry Music*. Boston: C. C. Birchard & Co., 1939, 1953.
2. Armitage, Theresa et al, *Our First Music*. Boston: C. C. Birchard & Co., 1941.
3. Armitage, Theresa et al, *Our Land of Song*. Boston: C. C. Birchard & Co., 1942, 1956.
4. Armitage, Theresa et al, *We Sing*. Boston: C. C. Birchard & Co., 1940, 1953.
5. Beattie, John W. et al, *American Singer*, Bk. I. New York: American Book Co., 1954.
6. Beattie, John W. et al, *American Singer*, Bk. II. New York: American Book Co., 1954.
7. Beattie, John W. et al, *American Singer*, Bk. III. New York: American Book Co., 1954.
8. Beattie, John W. et al, *American Singer*, Bk. IV. New York: American Book Co., 1954.
9. Beattie, John W. et al, *American Singer*, Bk. V. New York: American Book Co., 1956.
10. Hood, Marguerite and Schultz, Ernest J., *Learning Music Through Rhythm*. Boston: Ginn & Co., 1949.
11. Krone, Max, et al, *Music 'round the Clock*. Chicago: Follett Publishing Co., 1955.
12. McConathy, Osbourne et al, *New Music Horizons*, Bk. I. New York: Silver Burdett Co., 1944.
13. McConathy, Osbourne et al, *New Music Horizons*, Bk. II. New York: Silver Burdett Co., 1944.
14. McConathy, Osbourne et al, *New Music Horizons*, Bk. III. New York: Silver Burdett Co., 1944.
15. McConathy, Osbourne et al, *New Music Horizons*, Bk. IV. New York: Silver Burdett Co., 1945.
16. McConathy, Osbourne et al, *New Music Horizons*, Bk. V. New York: Silver Burdett Co., 1946.
17. Milne, A. A., *When We Were Very Young*. New York: E. P. Dutton & Co., Inc., 1924.
18. Mursell, James L. et al, *Music Through the Day*. New York: Silver Burdett Co., 1956.
19. Pitts, Lilla Belle et al, *The First Grade Book*. Boston: Ginn & Co., 1949.
20. Pitts, Lilla Belle et al, *The Kindergarten Book*. Boston: Ginn & Co., 1949.
21. Pitts, Lilla Belle et al, *Singing Every Day*. Boston: Ginn & Co., 1950.
22. Pitts, Lilla Belle et al, *Singing and Rhyming*. Boston: Ginn & Co., 1950.
23. Pitts, Lilla Belle et al, *Singing Together*. Boston: Ginn & Co., 1951.
24. Seeger, Ruth Crawford, *American Folk Songs for Children*. Garden City, New York: Doubleday & Co., Inc., 1948.
25. Zanzig, Augustus D., *Singing America*. Boston: C. C. Birchard & Co.

Additional References

Adams, Fay, *Educating America's Children*. New York: Ronald Press Co., 1946, pp. 415-420.

Andrews, Gladys, *Creative Rhythmic Movement for Children*. New York: Prentice-Hall, Inc., 1954.

Christianson, Helen, *Bodily Rhythmic Movements of Young Children in Relation to Rhythm in Music*. New York: Bureau of Publications, Teachers College, Columbia University, 1938.

Coleman, Satis, *Another Dancing Time* (contains music). New York: John Day Co., Inc., 1954.

Coleman, Satis, *Dancing Time* (Contains music). New York: John Day Co., Inc., 1952.

Driver, Ann, *Music and Movement*. London: Oxford University Press, 1936.

Dykema, Peter W. and Cundiff, Hannah M., *School Music Handbook*. Boston: C. C. Birchard & Co., 1955.

Flagg, Marion, *Musical Learning*. Boston: C. C. Birchard & Co., 1949, pp. 63-96.

Gehrkens, Karl W., *Music in the Grade*

Schools. Boston: C. C. Birchard & Co., 1934, pp. 25, 26, 41-42, 103-110.

Grant, Parks, *Music for Elementary Teachers*. New York: Appleton-Century-Crofts, Inc., 1951, Ch. V, XXIII.

Heffernan, Helen and California School Supervisors' Assn., *Guiding the Young Child*. Boston: D. C. Heath & Co., 1951.

Hughes, Langston, *The First Book of Rhythms*. New York: Franklin Watts, Inc., 1954.

Jersild, Arthur T. and Bienstock, Sylvia, *The Development of Rhythm in Young Children*. Child Development Monographs #22. New York: Bureau of Publications, Teachers College, Columbia University, 1935.

Krone, Beatrice Perham, *Music in the New School*. Chicago: Neil A. Kjos Music Co., 1947, pp. 91-106.

Landeck, Beatrice, *Children and Music*. New York: William Sloane Associates, 1952.

Lee, J. Murray and Lee, Dorris May, *The Child and His Curriculum*. New York: Appleton-Century-Crofts, Inc. (revised 1950), pp. 602-603.

Mathews, Paul Wentworth, *You Can Teach Music*. New York: E. P. Dutton & Co., Inc., 1953, Ch. V.

McConathy, Osbourne et al, *Music for Early Childhood*. New York: Silver Burdett Co., 1952, Ch. III.

Murray, Ruth Lovell, *Dance in Elementary Education*. New York: Harper & Bros., 1953.

Mursell, James L., *Education for Musical Growth*. Boston: Ginn & Co., 1948, pp. 4, 43-46, 76, 77, 182-183, 203-204.

Mursell, James L., *Music and the Classroom Teacher*. New York: Silver Burdett Co., 1951, Ch. IV.

Myers, Louise Kifer, *Teaching Children Music in the Elementary School*. New York: Prentice-Hall, Inc., 1956, Ch. IV.

Sheehy, Emma Dickson, *There's Music in Children*. New York: Henry Holt & Co., Inc., 1946, 1952.

*Waterman, Elizabeth, *Rhythm Book*. New York: A. S. Barnes & Co., 1937.

Wilson, Julie, "Dance Education for the Growing Child," *Journal of Health and Physical Education*, 19:5 (May, 1948), pp. 326-328, 381-383.

RECORDS

Bassett, Florence and Chesnut, Cora May, *Rhythmic Activities*. Children's Music Center, 2858 W. Pico St., Los Angeles, Calif.

Burns, Joseph et al, *Folk Dances* (instructions on records). Burns Record Co., 755 Chickadee Lane, Stratford, Conn.

Evans, Ruth, *Childhood Rhythms*, Series I, II, III, V, — Fundamental Rhythms; other Series — Folk Dances. Ruth Evans, 326 Forest Park Ave., Springfield, Mass.

James, Phoebe, *Phoebe James Rhythm Records AED 1-17*. Phoebe James, 746 46th Ave., San Francisco, Calif.

Methodist World of Fun, Folk Dances from all over the world. Nashville, Tenn.: Methodist Publishing House.

RCA Basic Elementary School Record Library, *Rhythmic Activities*. Vol. 1-6.

Square Dance Associates, *Honor Your Partner Series*. Graded square dances, 1 album for each grade I-V. Freeport, Long Island, N. Y.: Square Dance Associates.

FILMS

Woods, Lucille, *Holiday Rhythms*. Bowmar Records, 4921 Santa Monica Blvd., Los Angeles, California.

Woods, Lucille, *Rhythm Time*. Bowmar Records.

Building Children's Personalities with Creative Dancing. Los Angeles: University of California, Dept. of Cinema, color; available for sale or rental.

Rhythm Is Everywhere, Carl F. Mahnke Productions, 215 East Third St., Des Moines, Iowa.

*out of print

From bells to guitar

CHAPTER III

Let's Play Instruments

The use of instruments was mentioned in Chapter II, but the following suggestions are more detailed.

Many elementary schools have orchestras and bands. Most of these are taught by special music teachers. However, there are many interesting rhythm and pre-band instruments which the classroom teacher can use to advantage. Even the band and orchestral instruments can be used in the classroom.

¶ A MUSIC CENTER IN THE CLASSROOM — Each classroom should provide a music center, where the child may experiment with music as a free activity, and where he may come to recognize music as a pleasurable experience. Included in the music center might be:

Melody bells and sets of hard and of soft mallets
A drum and a few other rhythm instruments (assortment should
    be changed every few days)
An autoharp
Instruments created by the students or the teacher
Instruments brought in by the students
A bulletin board for
    Songs created by the children
    Pictures drawn by the children to illustrate songs
    Pictures drawn by the children to illustrate listening
    Musical current events and local programs clipped from
        newspapers and magazines
Books about music, instruments, composers
Song books

Rhythm Instruments

¶ CURRENT TRENDS IN THE USE OF RHYTHM INSTRUMENTS — At present writing the trend is away from the old type of rhythm band where primary children were drilled in performing on so-called rhythm instruments. The teacher told each child what to play and when to play it. The best players were given the most interesting instruments, and the *very* best player was exploited as the conductor. The band was uniformed, and played for Parent-Teacher Association meetings.

The fallacies of such a procedure are evident. The children became little robots performing the will of the teacher. Generally each child played the same instrument each time. Perhaps Johnny longed to try the drum, but was always given the sticks. Performance was the goal; the child was merely the medium.

The objectives of today are different. Rhythm instruments are used as tools for musical understanding. Children listen to music and decide what instruments are appropriate and when they should be played. Eventually they make their own instrumentation charts. They have opportunities to play different instruments, and the leader is not always the same child.

¶ WHAT CAN THE USE OF RHYTHM INSTRUMENTS DO FOR THE CHILD? — The use of instruments can

1. Give the child another means of enjoying music.
2. Give the child musical experience, other than singing, in which he can be successful.
3. Open up more opportunities for discriminative listening.
4. Help the child to develop his manipulative powers.
5. Develop the child's ability to form judgments.
6. Give the child another opportunity to work with others.
7. Lead the child to understand rhythmic notation.
8. Give the child another wedge into acceptance by the group.

¶ CLASSIFICATIONS OF RHYTHM INSTRUMENTS
By types of sound

Jingles and rings
    Triangles, jingle bells, finger cymbals, jingle clogs, cowbells, tambourines

Clicks
> Castanets, claves, sticks, temple blocks, wood blocks, tone gourds (struck)

Shakers
> Maracas, cabacas, pompons

Strokers
> Sand blocks, guiros, tone gourds (stroked), cabacas (twisted), xylophones (stroked)

Drums and tom-toms

Gongs and large cymbals

By volume

Loud
> Wood blocks, tone gourds, claves, castanets, temple blocks, large cymbals, drums

Soft
> Little jingle bells, triangles, finger cymbals, maracas, pompons, sand blocks, small sticks, chopsticks, soft beaters on large cymbals, gongs or drums.

By rhythmic pattern

Short sounds
> Sticks, wood blocks, claves, temple blocks

Long sounds
> Triangles, cymbals, gongs, bells, tambourines (shaken), xylophones (stroked)

Even and uneven rhythms
> Most instruments can be played either way, but castanets and maracas are especially adapted to uneven rhythms.

¶ EXPERIMENTATION WITH INSTRUMENTS — Children should be allowed ample opportunity to experiment with ways of playing instruments. Instruments should be accessible during school, free periods, recess, and after school. Children will find that drums can be struck on the heads (sides and center) and on the wood outside. Tambourines can be struck on the hand, the elbow or the knee, with beaters, and they can be shaken. Cymbals should be brushed together with a glancing stroke or tapped rather than clapped. Triangles ring if they are suspended from a string or holder instead of grasped tightly with the hand. A metal beater gives them a better tone than a wooden beater. Most instruments sound better if struck with a bouncing stroke, or as if one had touched a hot stove.

Experimentation may be followed by an identification game. The children close their eyes while one member of the class plays one of the instruments. The child who correctly names the instrument played becomes "it," and the game continues.

Occasionally a beginning teacher gives an instrument to each child before the children as a group have explored the sounds. Of course every child immediately starts experimenting with his own instrument. The resulting disturbance causes the teacher to conclude that the use of rhythm instruments is a college theory that is impractical in the classroom. Consequently her students are denied a very valuable and satisfying experience.

¶ INTRODUCTION OF RHYTHM INSTRUMENTS THROUGH SONGS — Some teachers like to introduce each instrument singly by teaching a song about the instrument and encouraging children to play that instrument to enrich the song. Care should be exercised that *all* children eventually have their chances to play. Suggested songs for this activity include

From *American Singer*, Bk. I (5)	
My Rhythm Sticks	p. 160
The Cymbals	161
My Tambourine	165
My Triangle	169
From *The First Grade Book* (19)	
Ring, Ring	173
Thumpity Drum	174
From *The Kindergarten Book* (20)	
Tip, Tip, Tap	138
The Triangle	138
The Drum	138
The Cymbals	138
From *Music Through the Day*	
Big Bass Drum	20
The Cymbals	18
My Tambourine	18

¶ USE OF INSTRUMENTS WITH FREE BODILY MOVEMENT — Some children enjoy using maracas, jingle bells, tambourines, and other instruments during free bodily movement. Music with strong rhythm encourages such activity. Ethnic records are particularly fine. The film, *Building Children's Personalities with Creative Dancing*, beautifully illustrates use of instruments during free response.

¶ RECOGNITION OF THE PRIMARY RHYTHMS — Children can learn to play walking, running and skipping music. A child selects a suitable instrument such as the drum to play walking music. Another plays running and another skipping music. One child may accompany another who is doing the bodily activity. (Care must be taken in selecting accompanists who will not confuse the child who is moving.)

Three different instruments may be selected by the children for the three primary rhythms. The *children* should be encouraged to experiment and to select instruments *suitable* for the pattern they wish to play. In this way they learn to discriminate. Suppose the children have chosen a drum for walking, sticks for running, and shakers for skipping. The "orchestra" listens as the teacher plays the piano or other instrument, and each member starts playing when he hears "his" music. Three small groups may also be ready to walk, run or skip when they hear the music. The rest of the class claps the rhythmic patterns. Care should be taken that all children are given opportunities to participate in all forms of activities. Those who clap at one time may walk, run, or skip the next, and play instruments another time.

As the children become more skillful in recognizing the primary rhythms, the teacher changes the music without warning, and the children play or stop playing accordingly.

Drum beat

¶ RESPONSE TO LONG NOTES (see p. 20) — In responding to long notes (𝅗𝅥   𝅗𝅥·   𝅝), children should select instruments with long sounds that carry over. (See p. 45.) One class selected the triangle for two-beat notes, the xylophone (stroked) for three-beat notes, and the cymbals for four-beat notes.

¶ RESPONSE TO THE RHYTHMIC PATTERN OF THE MELODY (see p. 20) — Experimentation will show the children which instruments are suitable for playing the rhythmic pattern of the melody of a song. Generally they select instruments which have a definite sound and are easy to play rapidly.

It is said that no sound pleases the human ear as much as the sound of one's own name. Children enjoy playing the rhythmic patterns of their names on rhythm instruments.

¶ RESPONSE TO THE UNDERLYING BEAT OR PULSE (see p. 20) — The children, with a little guidance, will decide that, since this rhythm is the same throughout, soft sounds such as those made by pompons, chopsticks, or sand blocks are appropriate.

¶ RESPONSE TO THE STRONG BEAT (See p. 21) — The very word *strong* guides the children to select suitable instruments. Inasmuch as the strong beat occurs less frequently than any other beat, speed of manipulation is not a consideration.

The more advanced groups can select loud instruments for the ONES, or accents, and soft instruments for the weak beats.

¶ COMBINING THE RHYTHMIC PATTERN OF THE MELODY, THE UNDERLYING PULSE AND THE STRONG BEAT. (See p. 23) — The children select three different kinds of instruments, one for playing the rhythmic pattern of the melody, another for the underlying pulse, and a third for the strong beats. Some of the children play while others respond with bodily activity. The rest of the class may clap.

¶ DISCOVERING PHRASES (See p. 23) — The class selects a different instrument for each phrase. An instrumentation chart such as the following helps children to remember their decisions each time the song is played.

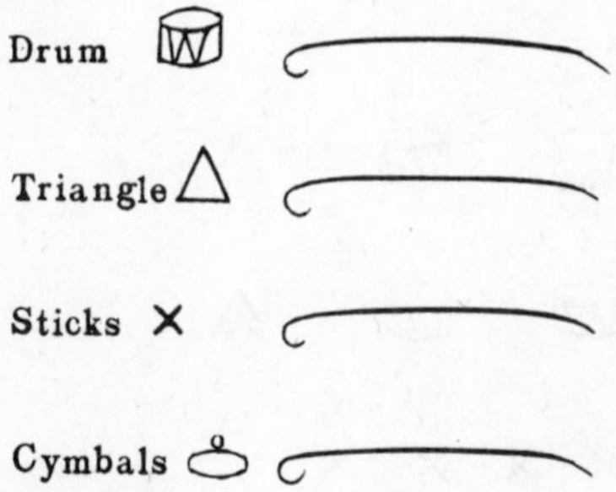

Drum   ⬚   ⌣‾‾‾‾‾

Triangle △   ⌣‾‾‾‾‾

Sticks ✗   ⌣‾‾‾‾‾

Cymbals ⌣   ⌣‾‾‾‾‾

¶ RECOGNITION OF LIKE AND UNLIKE PHRASES (p. 26) — Like instruments can be used for like phrases, and different instruments for different phrases. Children will think of ways to show similar phrases. *Example:*

Sticks   ✕ A

Finger Cymbals ◠◠ B

Sticks   ✕ A

Large Cymbals ◠ B′

¶ RESPONSE TO NOTATION (pp. 27, 28) — Children select a different instrument for each kind of note. *Example:*

♩   drum   🥁

♪   sticks   ✕

♩   triangle   △

Hot Cross Buns would be played:

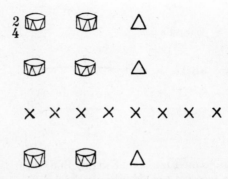

This type of activity applied to unfamiliar songs is a fine method of reading rhythmic notation.

¶ THE DOTTED QUARTER NOTE FOLLOWED BY THE EIGHTH (See p. 34) — One group of children plays the underlying pulse on instruments with soft sounds such as the sand blocks. At the same time another group plays the rhythmic pattern of the melody on instruments with definite sounds such as the claves. This activity shows that the dotted quarter note holds over through part of the second beat (actually has one and one-half beats).

¶ THE DOTTED QUARTER NOTE AS THE BEAT NOTE (See p. 35) — A different instrument may be selected for each group. *Example:*

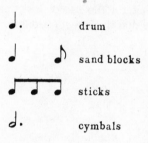

♩.   drum

♩   ♪   sand blocks

♩ ♩ ♩   sticks

♩.   cymbals

"See how they run" from *Three Blind Mice* would be played:

♩.   ♩   ♪ | ♩.

The rhythm of unfamiliar songs may be read by using instruments.

¶ SONG ENRICHMENT — Rhythm instruments may be used for song enrichment.

Some special effects children have used with songs include:

bells(church, telephone, etc.)	triangles, chimes, cymbals, jingle bells
rustling leaves	pompons, sand blocks
trains	sand blocks, whistles, tonettes

boat whistles	blowing across the tops of bottles
frogs	tone gourd, stroked very slowly
wooden shoes	wood blocks, temple blocks, sticks, claves
Latin-American instruments	maracas, guiros, drums (bongos, tumbas), castanets, claves, cabacas

Music 'round the Clock (9) and *Music Round the Town* (10) have many suggestions for the use of instruments to enrich songs. The authors intended that these suggestions be used as guides, rather than arbitrarily.

Rhythm Instruments

Rhythm and other instruments

Tonal Instruments

¶ CLASSIFICATIONS

Melody type
Melody bells or song bells
Resonator bells
Xylophones
Chimes
Tonettes, song flutes, flutophones, recorders
Ocarinas
Harmonicas
Psalteries
Piano
Organ (electric)

Accompaniment type
Autoharps
Harmolins
Ukeleles
Guitars
Piano
Harmonicas

Band and Orchestral Instruments
Violins
Violas*
Violoncellos
Double basses
Flutes
Piccolos*
Oboes*
Clarinets in B♭
English horns*
Bassoons*
Saxophones
       C melody
       E♭ alto
       B♭ tenor

* Rare in the average elementary school orchestra.

Eb baritone*
Trumpets in Bb
Cornets in Bb
French horns in F*
Alto horns in Eb
Mellophones in Eb and F
Trombones
Baritones
Tubas
Sousaphones

¶ WHAT CAN THE USE OF TONAL INSTRUMENTS DO FOR THE CHILD? — In addition to the list on page 44, the use of tonal instruments can

1. Lead the child to tonal discrimination, both in pitch and tone color, or timbre.
2. Develop the ability of the child to hear harmony.
3. Lead the child to an interest in the science of sound.
4. Develop the manipulative powers of the fingers.
5. Provide the child with a means of developing ability to read pitch in music.
6. Encourage students to learn to play instruments in bands and orchestras as well as individually.

Uses of Tonal Instruments

MELODY TYPE INSTRUMENTS

Melody bells, sometimes called *song bells,* or *chromatic bells,* are metal bars of varying lengths arranged scalewise and permanently fastened on a frame. Striking the bars with mallets produces the tone. Melody bells may be purchased in several sizes. Diatonic bells, one and a half octaves, are suitable for kindergartens, but for older children the two-octave chromatic type (having sharps and flats) are the most practical. It is important that bells be selected by a qualified person who knows pitch and tone quality. There are many makeshift, out-of-tune instruments on the market. These have no place in the schoolroom; every classroom should own a *good* set of bells.

Resonator bells (sometimes called *bell blocks*) are similar to melody bells except that each bar is fastened to a separate block, and the striking surface is larger. The larger striking surface is an advantage to the young child. Resonator bells have another advantage; each bell may be assigned to a different individual. Each child plays his bar when his note occurs in the melody. This technique may be used in teaching note reading.

Melode Bells are inexpensive sets of copper bells accurately tuned to the notes of the scale of F major. Each bell is concealed in a colored plastic bell with handle. The tone is produced by shaking. Each child holds one bell and plays it when his note occurs. Young children may play colored notation in which each note is colored to match the bell of corresponding pitch. Older children enjoy playing two- and three-part music. Three sets will equip each child in the average classroom.

Xylophones are similar to melody bells except that the bars are made of wood. Xylophones with a range of one octave are often found in kindergartens.

Chimes are metal tubes suspended from a frame and arranged according to the scale.

Melode bells

The Psaltery is a stringed instrument that is played by plucking. There is an eight-string psaltery for nursery school children, one with thirteen strings, and another with twenty-six strings for older children.

Any of the foregoing instruments can be used in the following ways:

¶ FOR EXPERIMENTATION — Children should have ample opportunity to experiment with instruments both in and out of school hours. Soft rubber mallets permit a child to play the bells without disturbing others.

¶ FOR CREATING ORIGINAL TUNES — Children should be encouraged to create their own tunes. The teacher should write some of them in line or standard notation. As the children progress, they can "help" the teacher. Some children can write their own tunes. A few have absolute pitch and are able to notate any melody they hear. These children can contribute a great deal to the class.

Children may write their original melodies in line notation, then change to standard notation.

¶ INTRODUCING THE CONCEPT OF HIGH AND LOW — Often a teacher tries diligently to help a child sing higher or lower, not realizing that the child may not know what is meant by higher or lower. To a child "high" is toward the sky, and "low" is toward the ground. However, on the piano, the harmonica, and the organ high is *right* and low is *left*. On the trombone high is *in* and low is *out*. On the tonette, the song flute, the flutophone, the recorder, or the clarinet high is *up* and low is *down*. On the 'cello and the double bass high is *down* and low is *up*, but right and left are also involved.

Some teachers approach the problem by standing the melody bells on end with the small bars up. In this way children learn to associate high pitch with high position and the short bars, and low pitch with low position and the long bars. Later these teachers ask the children to close their eyes and to show with their bodies when they hear high tones and when they hear low tones. The children stretch up for high and crouch down for low tones. A child can play the bells while the others respond with their bodies.

Other teachers introduce high and low by using a small bell of high pitch, and a large bell of low pitch. Resonator bells are good for this activity. A large bell can be used for playing Papa Bear's song, *Who's been sitting in my chair?* (11). A small one can be used for Baby Bear's, and a middle-sized bell for Mama Bear's song. This technique has a scientific basis, and can be used in constructing instruments. (See Chapter VI.)

One teacher made a large wooden rack and asked his pupils to bring various materials for chimes. For several weeks they had a set of chimes made from nails of different lengths. Later they used metal tubes, then flowerpots. Tuning glasses and bottles by using different amounts of water is an interesting project.

Examination of the psaltery, the autoharp, the harmolin, the different stringed instruments, and the inside of the piano shows that the longer the string the lower the pitch, and the thicker the string, the lower the pitch. The interior of a large pipe organ would interest many children. Teachers who do not capitalize upon the science of sound are missing an important opportunity.

Three Little Trains (Young People's Records) and *Penny Whistle* (Young People's Records) are records concerned with pitch. They are appropriate for primary children.

The film, *Science in the Orchestra,* is excellent and appropriate for all levels from primary to college.

¶ FOR SONG RECOGNITION — The teacher plays on a melody instrument an excerpt from a familiar song. The children name the song. Some of the children will be able to play some of the excerpts.

¶ FOR SONG ENRICHMENT — As the class sings a familiar song, a child may play an excerpt on the bells or other melody instrument. The teacher may show the starting point to young children. They continue by ear. Later they may play by note.

Descants and harmony parts may be played on melody instruments. Some teachers introduce a descant by playing it on the bells

Excerpts from familiar songs may be played as introductions and codas (endings) to the songs. Example from *Our Land of Song* (3):

The Little Pig   p. 123

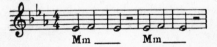

Mm ____   Mm____

¶ FOR INTRODUCTION OF NOTE READING — Easy songs may be written in line melodic notation for initial experiences in note reading. *Timothy's Tunes* by Adeline McCall (11), and *Stories That Sing* by Ethel Crowninshield (7) are good books for young children. In these books numbers are used to denote pitch. The lines in line notation are no longer on the same level as they were in line rhythmic notation; they are now higher or lower as the pitch goes up or down. If numbers are used in the music, numbers should be indicated on the instruments of pitch. Letters may be used if preferred.

Example 1   or   Example 2

3   B
    2   A
        1   G
Hot cross buns,   Hot cross buns,

3   B
    2   A
        1   G
Hot cross buns,   Hot cross buns,

        2 2 2 2   A A A A
1 1 1 1   G G G G
One a pen-ny, two a pen-ny, One a pen-ny, two a pen-ny,

3   B
    2   A
        1   G
Hot cross buns.   Hot cross buns.

Bells can be marked by nail polish or paint, but care must be exercised that the resonance is not deadened. One teacher placed numbered pieces of masking tape on the ends of the bars to identify them. When she wished to change keys, she merely pulled the first tape off and placed it in the new key. A child arranged the others to correspond.

A teacher in a kindergarten painted the end of each bell a different color. Then she placed colored dots below the words of familiar songs. The children played the songs by matching the colors of the bells to the dots. (There are sets of colored bells on the market.) These techniques may also be used on the electric organ or the piano.

There are many simple and interesting songs in the various school music books which may be used for further experiences in note reading.

¶ FOR PLAYING SONGS WHILE CHILDREN SING — A teacher who is not at ease in singing can learn to teach new songs by using the melody bells, the tonette, the piano, or other melody instrument. If the children can read, the words may be written on the board or followed in the books. Otherwise they can be repeated phrasewise by teacher, then pupils, before playing.

¶ FOR HELPING SINGERS — Some teachers ask a child to sing as he plays the melody bells. Often a non-singer will unconsciously find his singing voice by this activity.

¶ FOR STARTING SONGS — The teacher sounds the key note and, if necessary, the starting note for a song. She could ask a child to sound the notes. If the child cannot read music, the teacher must either tell him the names of the notes or have cards bearing suitable pictures for the songs, the names of the key notes and the initial notes. A child who is not particularly successful in other musical activities may take pride in starting songs.

MORE MELODY TYPE INSTRUMENTS

The Tonette is a small plastic instrument fingered with both hands and played by blowing into one end. The tone quality is similar to that of the flute, and the range is

The Song Flute is similar to the tonette, but somewhat smaller in diameter. Because it is smaller and the fingerholes conform to the shape of the hands, the young child may find it easier to play than the tonette. The tone quality is less brilliant than that of the tonette. The range is the same.

Note reading

The *Flutophone* is somewhat longer than the tonette and is shaped like a small clarinet. The end of it is flared or has a "bell" on it. An extra fingerhole permits the playing of

This note is not included in the range of the tonette and song flute. In tone quality and price the flutophone is similar to the tonette.

The *Recorder* is a more expensive instrument than the tonette. It has a better tone quality, and the range can be increased by over-blowing. The C-soprano and C-tenor recorders are non-transposing instruments, but the alto and bass recorders are built in the key of F. (See p. 71.) The teacher may enjoy the recorder for his own use.

Wind instruments owned by the school must be assigned to definite individuals and cleaned before re-assignment. Wood alcohol or commercial cleaning fluids may be used.

If the school does not provide instruments, their use involves expense. In some districts this is no problem. A mother in a less fortunate school was so impressed when she heard a group of tonette players from another school that she worked with the room-mothers to raise the money to buy them for the children who could not buy their own. The project was started after Christmas. Parents had been encouraged to give tonettes to their children as gifts at Christmas time.

One teacher° personally bought song flutes for each member of her class at the beginning of every school year. When she felt that a child played well enough, he was permitted to take his flute home to show his parents. Each child was told that his parents could purchase the instrument if they so desired. The teacher claims that she has never lost money on the "deal," and the children were motivated to learn in order that they might show their parents.

Some teachers who have felt insecure in the singing program have accomplished a great deal by teaching children in the third and fourth grades to play these instruments. *Melody Fun* (6) is a delightful little book for use with the tonette. It is cleverly illustrated. There are other good books listed in the bibliography.

One ingenious teacher°° made tonette bags similar to shoe-bags by stapling box-pleated pockets in manila tagboard. Each pocket was labeled, and the children kept their instruments in place when they were not in use.

Janet   Bob   Mary   Tom   Sue

° Miss Belle Piendl, teacher, first grade, Roosevelt School, Spokane, Washington.
°° Miss Christie Reierson, teacher, second grade, Franklin School, Spokane, Washington.

The Lyons Band Instrument Company, makers of the tonette, makes inexpensive individual cases. Room-mothers sometimes make them out of heavy cloth or plastic.

The Harmonica is generally played "by ear." It can also be played by a numbering system or by notes. Sometimes the letters D and B are added for "draw" and "blow," to indicate breathing. If the teacher enjoys playing and wants to give his class another medium of expression, there are some books on the market which can be of service. The Chromatic Harmonica is the most practical.

The Ocarina, often known as the "sweet potato," is a small clay or plastic instrument built on the same principle as the tonette, but held horizontally. There are a soprano, an alto, and a bass ocarina in the key of C. Other ocarinas are transposing instruments. (See p. 71.)

Guiding small hands

The Magnus Electric Organ is a small keyboard instrument with a two-octave range. It may be used for playing melodies or for chording. The keys are smaller than those on the piano.

The Piano can be used in the classroom in many different ways. Children can pick out tunes "by ear." They can play by the numbers, letters, or colors as they play the melody bells. (Keys can be marked.) Five-finger melodies such as *Mary Had a Little Lamb, Go Tell Aunt Rhodie,* and other simple songs can be played even by young children.

ACCOMPANIMENT INSTRUMENTS

The Autoharp is a stringed instrument suitable for playing chord accompaniments. It is not a melody instrument. The chords are formed by depressing the bars with the left hand, and strumming the strings with the right hand.

Autoharps are made with five, twelve, and fifteen bars. The 12-bar harp is used most commonly. It can be played in the keys of C, F, and G major and in d and a minor. The 15-bar harp is more expensive, but can be played in any key. Autoharps may be strummed on the Underlying Pulse, the Strong Beats, or occasionally on the Rhythmic Pattern of the Melody. Children should also be encouraged to experiment for other effects. Young children can strum while the teacher presses the bars. For many songs the children can decide which chords to use, and the teacher can chart them on cards for the use of the students.

¶ PROCEDURE — As the class sings a familiar song, the teacher or a pupil strums the Tonic (I) chord until the class objects to its sound. Then the Dominant Seventh (V^7) chord can be tried. If neither of these chords pleases the students, the Sub-dominant (IV) chord may be tried. The song continues until the class desires another change of chord, and so on. If neither the I, the V^7, or the IV chord seems to satisfy the class, a child may volunteer to experiment and search for the "lost chord."

¶ CHARTING A SONG ACCOMPANIMENT — Chord changes may be charted as follows:

MARY HAD A LITTLE LAMB

Key of G   Starting note — B

$\frac{2}{4}$ | **G**
Mar-y   had   a | lit - tle   lamb,

D7
|Lit - tle   lamb, | **G**
lit - tle   lamb,

G
|Mar-y   had   a | lit - tle   lamb,

D7
Its |fleece was white as | **G**
snow.

The Harmolin is another chording instrument. It is played by strumming. It can be adjusted to any key, but is more expensive than the autoharp.

The Ukelele is a simple, inexpensive instrument which many children own. Its four strings can be tuned in two ways.

When the ukelele is tuned by method 1, it can be played easily in the keys of F, C, and G. When tuned by method 2, it can be played easily in the keys of G, D, and A. Although experts can play melodies on the ukelele, the average player plays only chords.

The fingerboard is marked off by thin horizontal metal bars called *frets*. Pressing the fingers of the left hand between the frets determines the pitch. Each fret, counting from the peg box to the body, raises the pitch of a string by one-half step. A small guitar of Portuguese origin, the ukelele is now considered the national instrument of The Islands. The name, "ukelele," is a combination of the Hawaiian *uku,* insect, and *lele,* to jump — from the movement of the fingers in playing (15). The ukelele is played by the right hand strumming up and down across the strings. Children enjoy playing the instrument, especially to accompany Hawaiian songs. Song charts showing suitable chords are useful (see p. 65). Some songs have miniature chord fingerings for the ukelele printed above the music (1:11, 3:91).

The Latin Americans have a similar instrument called the *cuatro.* It is slightly larger than the ukelele and sounds lower. It is tuned like the ukelele with the exception of the first and the fourth strings, which are tuned an octave lower than those of the ukelele.

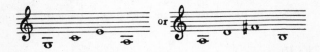

The Guitar is another fretted instrument similar to the ukelele but larger. The four-stringed guitar can be played like the ukelele, but the six-stringed Spanish guitar is more complicated. A teacher who can play the guitar should most certainly use it. It is a fine instrument for accompanying both singing and rhythmic movement. Both melody and chords can be played by an expert. This is also the case with the Hawaiian steel guitar. Some guitars are electrically amplified. Students who play guitars should be encouraged to play for the class.

The Piano or the *Electric Organ* can be used to accompany both singing and rhythmic activities. Children in the general classroom can learn to play the I, IV, and V⁷ chords. The following chords in the key of C are easily transposed to other keys:

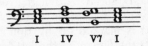

     I   IV   V7   I

BAND AND ORCHESTRAL INSTRUMENTS

Band and orchestral instruments, in addition to the uses listed on pages 44 and 55, can

1. Provide the child with a first-hand acquaintance with the instruments of the band and the orchestra.
2. Lead the child to recognition of the tone colors of the different instruments.
3. Give the child an opportunity to try playing some of these instruments.
4. Open a wider field for the study of the science of sound.

Many children in the elementary school take private or class lessons on band and orchestral instruments. These children can contribute to the music of the general classroom. They should be encouraged to bring their instruments, explain them, and demonstrate them to the class. They can play the melodies of songs the class sings, and they can play descants or harmony parts.

Occasionally a classroom teacher asks a child to play his instrument in class and is then puzzled because the instrument sounds "out-of-tune." This may be because the instrument is a *transposing instrument,* that is, it sounds a note different from the same note played on the piano.

The piano, violin, 'cello, double bass, C flute, C saxophone, B♭ trombone (bass clef), and tuba (bass clef) sound C when playing C. Other instruments vary, and will be discussed later. (See p. 71.)

¶ STRINGED INSTRUMENTS — Stringed instruments can be used effectively by children who have had no lessons. The classroom teacher should know something about them, but she need not hesitate to ask the students who play them for more specific information.

The Double Bass (string bass) is the largest of the stringed instruments. The player stands and balances his instrument against his left knee. He fingers the strings with his left hand, and with his right draws the bow across the strings. He may also pluck the strings. This method of playing is called "pizzicato" (pit-si-kah'to), and is used extensively in dance bands.

The four strings are tuned thus:

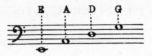

The strings sound an octave lower than the music is written.

Children enjoy seeing and playing the double bass. Any child can play pizzicato with the forefinger of his right hand. Pulling the string at an angle prevents it from slapping against the fingerboard.

A bass for songs in the keys of G Major or g minor can be played using the G string for the I chord, the D string for the V^7 chord, and the E or the G for the IV chord (contained in the chord CEG).

A happy trio

The keys of D and A can also be used in a similar manner.

I	V⁷	IV
D	A	G
A	E	D

The Violoncello is commonly known as the *'cello* (pronounced chello). It is somewhat smaller than the double bass. The player is seated and holds the instrument between his knees.

The strings are tuned thus:

The strings corresponding to the suitable chords may be plucked. The keys of G, D, and C can be used.

I	V⁷	IV
G	D	C
D	A	G
C	G	A or C (from FAC)

The Viola is similar to the violin but larger. It plays a part lower than the violin. Because of its size it is not usually played by children in the elementary school. It is held under the chin like the violin, and is tuned an octave higher than the 'cello. It uses an alto clef rather than the treble or bass clef. Occasionally an elementary child learns to play the viola on a violin strung like a viola. Because it is not used in many elementary schools, the viola will not be discussed further.

The Violin is the smallest stringed instrument used in the orchestra. It is held under the left side of the chin. It is tuned thus:

Concentration

*Awaiting
the cue*

Notice that the strings are just the reverse of those on the double bass (EADG), but sound much higher. The chords used for the double bass can also be used with the violin.

¶ WIND INSTRUMENTS — Some *wind* instruments can be used to play the music as it is written and they will be in the same key as the piano and the voice. These instruments are the C flute, the C melody saxophone, the oboe, the C piccolo, the trombone, and the tuba. (The music for the trombone and the tuba must be written in the bass clef.)

¶ TRANSPOSING INSTRUMENTS — The B♭ clarinets, trumpets, cornets, tenor saxophones, and trombones (treble clef) are *transposing* instruments. When playing C they sound B♭, a tone lower than C. Since they sound a tone lower than the written music, it will be necessary to write their music one whole tone *higher* in order for them to play in tune with the piano, the violin and other C instruments. If a B♭ clarinet, trumpet, or cornet is played while the class sings, one of two things must happen. Either the class must sing the song one tone lower, or the player must transpose his music one tone higher than the music in the song books.

The music for E♭ instruments, such as the E♭ alto horn, the E♭ alto saxophone, and the mellophone (E♭), must be rewritten a major sixth higher. That for the French horn (F) must be rewritten a perfect fifth higher. If this is not done, the players must transpose the music when playing as the class sings.

Music written sounds

Music Across Our Country (8) gives many suggestions for the use of instruments with songs.

The use of the actual instruments in the classroom is far superior to the old method of showing pictures and playing records. It is even more meaningful than a film because it is a real experience. This experience is a live lesson in appreciation and can also contribute a great deal toward the science lesson. Size and length of tube and string, effect of materials (metal and wood), effect of reeds, and air chambers offer many opportunities. Fingers closing holes lengthen a tube and lower the pitch. Fingers on strings shorten the length and raise the pitch. Of course the use of recordings along with the instruments makes an even fuller experience. (See Chapter V.)

Questions for Class Discussion

1. Distinguish between the modern use of rhythm instruments and the old rhythm band.
2. Do you believe children should be allowed to play "by ear"? Why, or why not?
3. What contributions can the playing of instruments make toward music reading activities?
4. Discuss this statement: "It is a waste of time to play pre-band instruments; children should start on real instruments."
5. List the rhythm instruments and the number of each you would buy for a specific grade of your choice.
6. List the melody instruments you would buy (in order of importance).
7. What chording instruments would you buy?
8. What points should be considered in selecting instruments?

More concentration

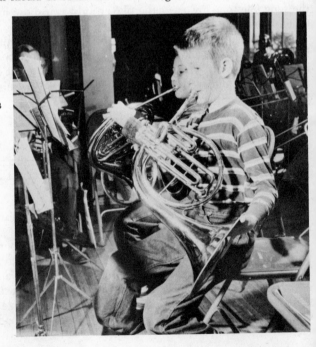

Explanation

Wind in the trees

Bibliography

1. Armitage, Theresa et al, *Music Everywhere*. Boston: C. C. Birchard & Co., 1943, 1955.
2. Armitage, Theresa et al, *Our First Music*. Boston: C. C. Birchard & Co., 1941.
3. Armitage, Theresa et al, *Our Land of Song*. Boston: C. C. Birchard & Co., 1942.
4. Armitage, Theresa et al, *Our Songs*. Boston: C. C. Birchard & Co., 1939, 1952.
5. Beattie, John W. et al, *American Singer*, Bk. I. New York: American Book Co., 1954.
6. Buchtel, Forrest L., *Melody Fun*. Chicago: Lyons Band Instrument Co., 1938.
7. Crowninshield, Ethel, *Stories that Sing*. Boston: Boston Music Co., 1945.
8. Krone, Max et al, *Music Across Our Country*. Chicago: Follett Pub. Co., 1956.
9. Krone, Max et al, *Music 'round the Clock*. Chicago: Follett Pub. Co., 1955.
10. Krone, Max et al, *Music Round the Town*. Chicago: Follett Pub. Co., 1955.
11. McCall, Adeline, *Timothy's Tunes*. Boston: Boston Music Co., 1943.
12. Mursell, James L. et al, *Music Through the Day*. New York: Silver Burdett Co., 1956.
13. Pitts, Lilla Belle et al, *The First Grade Book*. Boston: Ginn & Co., 1949.
14. Pitts, Lilla Belle et al, *The Kindergarten Book*. Boston: Ginn & Co., 1949.
15. Webster, Noah, *Webster's Collegiate Dictionary*. Springfield, Mass.: G. & C. Merriam Co.

Additional References

Adams, Fay, *Educating America's Children*. New York: Ronald Press, 1946, pp. 412-414.

Bishop, Dorothy, *Chords in Action*. New York: Carl Fischer, Inc., 1956 (for the teacher).

Carabo-Cone, Madeline and Royt, Beatrice, *How to Help Children Learn Music*. New York: Harper & Bros., 1953.

Coleman, Satis, *Your Child's Music*. New York: John Day Co., Inc., 1939, Ch. V.

Davis, Dorothy, *Autoharp Accompaniments for Music Everywhere*. Boston: C. C. Birchard & Co., 1955.

DuBois, Charlotte, *Songs to Play*. Boston: C. C. Birchard & Co., 1954.

Dykema, Peter W. and Cundiff, Hannah M., *School Music Handbook*. Boston: C. C. Birchard & Co., 1955.

Fox, Lillian Mohr, *Autoharp Accompaniments to Old Favorite Songs*. Boston: C. C. Birchard & Co., 1947.

Frisch, Fay Templeton, *The Play-Way to Music Series* for piano instruction. New York: Leo Feist, Inc., 1954.

Hood, Marguerite and Schultz, Ernest J., *Learning Music Through Rhythm*. Boston: Ginn & Co., 1949.

Katz, Erich, *Recorder Playing* (for F and C recorders). New York: Clark and Way, Inc., 1951.

Krone, Beatrice Perham, *Music in the New School*. Chicago: Neil A. Kjos Music Co., 1947.

Krone, Beatrice and Max, *Harmony Fun with the Autoharp*. Chicago: Neil A. Kjos Music Co., 1952.

Mathews, Paul W., *You Can Teach Music*. New York: E. P. Dutton & Co., 1953, Ch. VII.

McKenzie, Clemewell, *Before We Join the Band*. New York: Mills Music Co., 1948.

McLaughlin, Roberta and Dawley, Muriel, *Sing and Play with the Autoharp*. 2858 W. Pico St., Los Angeles, Calif.: Children's Music Center.

Morgan, Hazel Nohavec, *Music in American Education*. Washington, D.C.: Music Educators National Conference, 1955, pp. 163-171, 174-192, 309-312.

Mursell, James L., *Education for Musical*

Growth. Boston: Ginn & Co., 1948.

Mursell, James L., *Music and the Classroom Teacher.* New York: Silver Burdett Co., 1951, Ch. VII.

Myers, Louise Kifer, *Teaching Children Music in the Elementary School.* New York: Prentice-Hall, Inc., 1956, pp. 49, 50, 63, 64, 73, 206-208.

Nelson, Mary Jarman, *Fun with Music.* Chicago: Albert Whitman & Co., 1941.

Pace, Robert, *Piano for the Classroom.* Englewood Cliffs, N. J.: Prentice-Hall, Inc., 1956. (For the Teacher.)

Slind, Lloyd H., *The Play and Sing Book.* Boston: C. C. Birchard & Co., 1956.

*Thomas, Max, *Play Time* (Tonette method). Chicago: Neil A. Kjos Music Co., 1938.

Timmerman, Maurine, "Miss Brown Teaches the Class Piano," *Music Educators Journal,* Nov.-Dec. 1949, pp. 16-17.

Timmerman, Maurine, "Instruments in the General Classroom," *Music Educators Journal,* Apr. 1952.

Trapp Family Singers, *Enjoy Your Recorder,* Bk. M-1 for C-Soprano or C-Tenor; Bk. M-2 for F-Alto, F-Sopranino, or F-Bass. Garrison, N. Y.: Magnamusic Distributors, Inc., 1954.

---

out of print

FILMS

Autoharp, The, Johnson-Hunt Co., 6509 DeLongpre Ave., Hollywood 28, Calif.. 1955. 1 reel, 20 min.

Children's Concert, Encyclopaedia Britannica Films, Inc., 1950. 3 reels, 10-12 min. per reel.

Building Children's Personalities with Creative Dancing, Cinema Dept., University of California, Los Angeles, Cal., 1954. 1 reel.

Instruments of the Orchestra, British Information Service, 1947. 20 min.

Keyboard Experiences in Classroom Music No. 8. Bureau of Publications, Teachers College, Columbia University, New York, N.Y.

Little Fugue in G Minor — Bach, Teaching Films Custodians, 1951. 4 min.

Music with the Melode Bells, Dow Chemical Co., Midland, Mich.

Rhythm Instruments and Movement, Encyclopaedia Britannica Films. 1 reel, 10 min. For primary grades.

Science in the Orchestra, British Information Service, 1951. 3 reels, 35 min.

Singing Pipes, Canadian National Film Board, 1947. 22 min.

Sounds of Music, Coronet, 1948. 10 min

Story of a Violin, The, National Film Board of Canada, 1948. 21 min.

Playing characteristic themes

CHAPTER IV

Let's Sing

Singing is a natural means of expression for the small child, who often sings before he talks. He sings at play and at other activities. Most of his songs are his own improvisations created at the moment to fit his particular need.

When he enters school, music must continue as a free and natural means of expression for him. Frequently he will engage in spontaneous singing at work or at play, before and during rest periods, and during story time. Such informal singing encourages the child to express himself imaginatively and without self-consciousness.

Singing experiences in the elementary school should include informal music, both inside and outside the group. This music may be integrated with social studies, science, and language arts, or it may be purely recreational and for release from tension. Aside from the informal experiences there should also be a special time set aside for music. This should be a short concentrated period with music as the main point of emphasis. Any mastery of technique should contribute toward both the musical development and the happiness of the child.

Singing can scarcely be dissociated from other musical experiences. Rhythmic, creative and listening experiences should be inseparable from singing. Kindergarten offers the opportunity to open up the world of music to the young child through varied media, so that he may sing and dance as easily as he speaks. Contact with music needs to be free, natural, and easy rather than technical.

It is hoped that the teacher will feel that the procedures in-

cluded in this section on singing experiences are not mandatory, but
rather the starting point of growth in the teaching of music. Some
interesting experimental work is now in progress, and there is need
for more.

¶ WHAT CAN SINGING DO FOR THE CHILD? — The teacher is encouraged to strive constantly for new and effective approaches in
order to
1. Help each child to find his singing voice.
2. Help children feel and interpret the mood of songs.
3. Provide singing as a means of self-expression.
4. Develop the ability to sing smoothly and with good enunciation.
5. Make music meaningful in other areas.
6. Cause pupils to enjoy their music so much that they will
   always want more of it. They should feel the need of it
   throughout the day, in work or play, in or out of school.

All of the above contribute toward those most important mo-
tives of children, desire for social approval, mastery of subject, need
for new experience, and desire for security and individuality.

¶ THE TEACHER'S VOICE — The teacher's voice necessarily affects the quality of the voices of the children. A highly cultivated
voice is not necessary, but pleasing tone quality, accurate pitch, and
enjoyment of singing are. Facial expression should reflect the mood
of the song.

Unless the teacher has perfect pitch, it is best to use the pitch
pipe, the piano, the organ, the autoharp, or the bells for the initial
note of each song. If the teacher has an inadequate singing voice,
she can (with care) teach rote songs by the use of melody instruments or recordings. (See p. 60.) The latter limits the choice of
material, however. Not all recordings are suitable. Children enjoy
and understand a good folk singer better than an operatic singer.
Some of the songs from school texts are available on records. However, the teacher should make every effort to learn to sing well
enough to teach the songs herself. (See p. 86) for suggestions for
teaching rote songs.)

If a teacher finds a song too high for her voice she should not
hesitate to transpose it to a more comfortable key. Transposition is
not difficult. Suppose the teacher wants to teach *Echo Song* (1:56).
The song is written in the key of F major. The highest note in the

song is . Miss Brown knows the song, but cannot reach the high F. She decides to transpose the song a third lower to the key of D major; then her highest note will be D. Since the starting note was originally C, she must transpose it down a third to A. She sounds the new keynote D, the new starting note A, and proceeds with the song. (If Miss Brown plays the song on the bells, the piano or other instrument, she must play every note in the song a third lower than it is written, and she must remember that there are two sharps in the key of D major.) The children learn the song in Miss Brown's key but find the low notes too low for them. After they have the melody well in mind, Miss Brown gives the pitch in the original key, and the children carry on.

A man should sing in his own register. (Children often learn to sing from their fathers.) Occasionally a young child tries to imitate a bass voice, but not often. If a child does try to imitate a male voice, the teacher may play a little of the melody on the piano or the melody bells to show the child the pitch at which he should sing. Sometimes another child can help at this point.

When a song is first presented to children, it should be sung by the teacher with clear enunciation. However, diction should not be *over-emphasized* to the extent that the rhythm is distorted. If the word content is understood, the children's voices will reflect the beauty and mood of the song they are singing. A song may be happy, sad, quiet, thoughtful, animated, or playful.

The teacher should sing rhythmically with a steady floating tone. The intensity and tempo of the song should be given the children when it is *first* sung, rather than after it has been sung many times.

Phrases and words should not be broken in the middle by breathing. The thought and meaning of a phrase should be respected the same in singing as in speaking. A breath is the same as a punctuation mark. Children will imitate the teacher in this respect.

¶ THE VOICE OF THE YOUNG CHILD — Good tone quality is clear, unforced, resonant, free from breathiness, and capable of being sustained with little effort. It is seldom hushed, but never raucous. It is the result of interpretation of the mood and meaning of the song. An appeal to the imagination of the children will usually get the desired effect. "Would your baby brother fall asleep if he heard you singing the song as you did?" is a better approach than, "Sing softly." Or "How do you think we should sing this song?" and "Why?" are better than, "This is a lively song. Sing it faster."

¶ THE RANGE OF THE CHILD VOICE — The range of the voice of the average young child is from Middle C to C, D, or E above. Most nursery school children cannot be expected to have a range that wide. There are some songs (such as *Mary Had a Little Lamb*) with a span of five tones which are suitable for beginners. Because research concerning the child voice is rather recent, some songs are written too high for children. For this reason it is important to understand transposition.

¶ THE SINGING VOICE — Inability to sing may be the result of lack of experience with pitch, of inattention, or of an emotional block. The latter is a very common cause. Only in rare instances does one find a child with a physical defect which prevents his singing. Research indicates that children's singing voices can be improved by training.

The very young child can be helped without embarrassment to him. Helping the older child is more difficult. No youngster should feel ashamed of the fact that he encounters difficulty in singing, but he should realize that he needs help. He should feel that his teacher and his classmates are trying to assist him. The good teacher will tolerate neither ridicule nor laughter from the class when a child is having difficulty.

It is well to develop a feeling of pride among all pupils when one of them shows improvement. Many adults can trace their inability to sing to some embarrassment during early childhood. (See Chapter I.)

Individual help should be given daily. Play offers excellent opportunities to help children to sing. Often a child will unconsciously call in a high voice during a game. A good teacher will capitalize upon this at the time. Praise is very important.

Developing Pitch Consciousness

Most children will match tones within a comparatively short time, but others will require months of individual help. The teacher must be alert at all times for new ways to reach a child. Children can invent games and dramatizations which will help. Sometimes a few minutes with a child alone before or after school will be rewarding. Some children respond to large intervals better, others respond to small ones. Raising and lowering the hand as in line notation (p. 59) helps some children.

Although most of this development of pitch consciousness takes place in the primary grades, occasionally a child will reach the intermediate or upper grades without finding his singing voice. In that case it is the business of both the classroom teacher and the special teacher to help the child tactfully, outside of the class.

Failure to find his singing voice excludes the child from one area of musical participation. Occasionally a boy finds his singing voice when his voice changes, but it is unfortunate if he misses singing prior to adolescence.

Singing is a personal activity. This may be because it comes directly from the body. No tools are used. It can be heard, and it is almost certain to please or to displease others. Telling a person he cannot sing has an effect comparable to telling him he is ugly. For that reason the teacher must be exceedingly tactful in helping the child, yet help him she must. At the same time she must remember that if he becomes tense, this will defeat her purpose. Rather she must give the child the feeling that he is successful in music. Little activities such as numbering or lettering phrases in songs (pp. 24, 26) contribute toward a feeling of success. Bodily activity, playing instruments, listening, all contribute toward the whole. Success in any of these areas helps the child to relax, and this helps him to find his singing voice. Recent research and experiments indicate that bodily awareness (12) plays a major role in singing.

It seems that the singing of high and low is a *physical sensation* in many cases, rather than a matter of hearing. There is need for more experimentation in this area of research.

¶ PLAYING HIGH AND LOW (See p. 57) — An important initial activity is development of the concept of high and low. This may be followed by songs such as:

American Singer, I (7)

The Slide	p. 17
Swinging High, Swinging Low	139
Icicles	171

Swing high!

Some teachers ask the children to accompany these songs by bodily response; others object to such activity because they feel that it causes tension when singing high tones.

¶ SINGING AND PLAYING — Some children subconsciously develop ability to match tones by singing as they play songs, or excerpts from songs, on the melody bells, the psaltery, the organ, or the piano. Examples:

"came rolling home" from "This Old Man"
    The First Grade Book (33:44)
    Music Round the Town (21:106)

"ten little Indian boys" from "Ten Little Indians"
    The American Singer, Bk. I (7:94)

"Oh, how I like to go round,
All day long on the merry-go-round."
    Music Through the Day (31:105)

"you and I" from "In School Together"
    Our First Music (3:5)

¶ MATCHING INITIAL TONES OF A SONG — Some children can sing with the group only if they find the initial tone of the song. After sounding this tone, the teacher should take a few minutes to help these children locate it before the class begins to sing.

¶ SINGING SONGS ON THEIR OWN PITCH LEVEL — Occasionally a child who cannot sing with the group can sing the song perfectly when permitted to start on his own pitch. Success in singing the song for the class gives him a feeling of security. The teacher may then try to start him one tone higher or lower than his own pitch. Praise always helps.

¶ SINGING CONVERSATIONS — The teacher sings questions to the children about things in the room, things seen on the way to school, pets, or things done in school. Questions should be phrased so that the answers will require complete sentences rather than "Yes" or "No." Pupils create their own tunes in answering. Some children who cannot reproduce a given melody can sing when creating their own songs.

¶ DRAMATIZATION

Playing Telephone
    This game is the same as singing conversations except that two

children sing to each other over toy or imaginary telephones.

Riding the Elevator

The "operator" calls the floors, raising the pitch of his voice as he calls each higher floor, and lowering it as he calls the lower floors. Children should be encouraged to create their own words. One class dramatized it thus:

Operator "First floor, candy,"
"Second floor, ice-cream,"
"Third floor, toys,"
"Fourth floor, cowboy boots."

Customers entered the elevator on different floors calling, "In, please" to match the tones of the operator, and departed calling, "Out, please." This game was part of the unit "Community Helpers."

Piloting an Airplane

Children sometimes find their singing voices by sounding like an airplane flying high over a mountain.

Playing Train

A child sounds the train whistle with his voice. He then chooses another child to match his "whistle." The remainder of the class judges whether the "whistles are the same" or not. If the second child matches the first, he may hitch on to the engine. Other children are added in the same manner. Five or six cars are sufficient for one train. The remainder of the class sounds "choo-choo-choo-choo" as the train travels around the room. Sand blocks may also be used for sound effects. To avoid hurt feelings, the unsuccessful child may occasionally sound the whistle the other children must match. However, he must continue his efforts to find his singing voice.

Stop the Music (See p. 20)

This game may also be used for helping the individual child with his singing voice. The child who is "it" sings the first phrase of a familiar song with "loo" or other neutral syllable. Another child names the song. If he is successful, the class sings the song and he sings the first phrase of another familiar song. If he is unsuccessful, another child tries, and the game continues. The teacher helps the one who is "it" by singing with him if necessary.

The foregoing techniques are only a few possibilities for helping children to find their singing voices. Teachers must be alert to opportunities at all times. They should acquire the habit of sharing ideas with each other.

¶ PROGRESS CHART — Many teachers of primary children find a progress chart encouraging to *themselves*. They list the pupils in columns according to ability and move them as they progress.

Suggested classifications are:

1. Those who cannot match a tone.
2. Those who can match a tone, but cannot sing a tune.
3. Those who can sing with the group.
4. Those who can sing independently.

The children should *not* see this chart.

Seating Arrangements

Whether specific seating should be used in arranging a music class must be answered by the individual teacher. Children should not be aware of the fact they are grouped according to singing ability. (See Chapter I.)

Various factors in the classroom will determine which type of music class arrangement a teacher chooses for a group — number of children, availability of an accompanying instrument, time to be devoted to the musical activity, type of activity, and physical facilities of the room. Variety in the seating arrangement of a music class at various times will add interest.

Suggested arrangements are:

1. Group the class informally around the piano (either on chairs or on the floor), or group the children informally around the teacher who is sitting so that she is on the eye level of the children.
2. Place the independent singers near those who need help.
3. Seat the better singers at the back and the weaker near the teacher so that she may easily help them. (Children should *not* be aware of this grouping.)
4. Group the children in a circle or a semi-circle. This plan would be effective with the smaller groups.
5. Seat the children according to the parts they sing when part singing is introduced. (See page 107.)
6. Allow the children to sit wherever they happen to be when the music period starts. At all times children should be seated within the eye span of the teacher.

Choice of Songs

The melody of each song should be pleasing. If it is not melodious enough for the teacher to remember overnight, it may not be worth teaching.

Selection of songs should be made with consideration of the child's experience and his immediate interest. A song about rain is more effective if taught on a rainy day. Pictures, stories, and concrete objects may be used as motivation, but *the song itself* should be sufficiently interesting to hold the attention of the class. If they like them, children will learn very intricate songs from radio and television. One student teacher who was inclined to spend too much time on motivation learned a lesson from her young son at home. She was practicing her presentation of a rote song and had spent considerable time building up to the moment when she would sing the song. Suddenly she was interrupted by this remark, "Hey, Mom! Cut out the corn and let's get on with the song!"

The attention span of a young child is very short. His songs should be short, and he should learn many of them. Older children like longer songs. They will not be able to learn as many, because their songs will be not only longer but more difficult.

Until some of the voices begin to change, the songs should be ranged between Middle C and fourth space E. An occasional F is permissible.

There should be variety in the choice of songs. Patriotic songs, folk songs, community songs, experience songs, songs of the holidays and seasons, lullabies, humorous songs, singing games, hymns, and some songs in other languages should be included (43:62). An occasional popular song is suitable for children. *Rudolph, the Red-nosed Reindeer, The Easter Parade,* and *White Christmas* were songs of this type.

Methods of Teaching a Song

A rote song is taught by imitation. It is helpful for the teacher to sing the entire song in a distinct and pleasing manner each day for a few days before attempting to teach the song to the children.

¶ PARTICIPATION METHOD — In songs with easy, recurring phrases the children should be encouraged to join the teacher in singing those phrases as soon as they can. Examples:

"Heave away, heave away!" from
American Singer, V   (11:42)

"O, yes!" from "John the Rabbit"
New Music Horizons, IV   (28:120)

Animal sounds and "Cat goes fiddle-i-dee" from
"The Barnyard Song," *Our First Music*   (3:149)

"Ho hum, gone to his grave," from
"Old Roger Is Dead," *Singing and Rhyming*   (40:51)

After singing the song several times in this way the class will be
able to sing the entire song, the teacher singing only when needed.

One teacher applies the participation method in a slightly different manner. He sings the entire song several times and the class
discusses the word content. Then the teacher sings the song omit-
ting the ends of phrases. The children fill in when he stops. This
keeps the class alert; at the same time they are hearing the song
again before attempting the entire song. The teacher then gradually
withdraws as the class is able to sing the whole song.

¶ DRAMATIZATION METHOD — Children may listen to the song,
discuss it, and respond to it rhythmically, or dramatize it. By the

*"Rabbits come out of silk hats, but
dragons come out of laundry bags."*

time they have listened to it a number of times and dramatized it, they will know the words and the melody. Examples:

A Paper of Pins	*American Singer*, III	(9:144)
Ball Games	*Merry Music*	(1:27)
The Gardener	*Music 'round the Clock*	(20:18)
Folk Dance	*New Music Horizons*, IV	(28:16)
The Bus	*Singing and Rhyming*	(40:10)
The Barnyard Song	*Our First Music*	(3:149)
Farmyard Song	*New Music Horizons*, IV	(28:102)
I Had Four Brothers	*Our Land of Song*	(4:118)

¶ For a Short Song — After the teacher has sung the song on several successive days, the teacher and the children sing it together in its entirety. Then the children try it alone.

¶ For a Long Song — Work proceeds as for a short song, but phrases giving difficulty are used in drill. The teacher sings them and pupils repeat. Then pupils and teacher sing the song together. Finally the pupils try it alone, the teacher helping when needed.

Some teach a long song phrasewise. That is, the pupils imitate the teacher's singing of each individual phrase. Then two phrases are joined by the teacher and imitated by the pupils. Finally the whole song is sung. The teacher who uses this method may lose the pitch occasionally, or she may lose the continuity of the song. She may also waste time drilling on phrases which need no drill.

¶ Using the Flannel Board — The flannel board is useful in teaching some songs. Different characters may be pictured and placed on the board as the teacher sings. In this way, the class participates and learns the sequence while hearing the song sung several times by the teacher.

¶ Using the Piano or the Chromatic Bells (if the teacher does not sing) — One teacher plays the entire song. Then she repeats the words. If the children can, they may read the words from books or the chalkboard.

Then the teacher repeats the words of the first phrase as she plays the piano. The children sing the phrase with the piano, then without the piano. This procedure is repeated for each phrase. The children sing the whole song with the piano and finally without it.

Chromatic bells or organ may be used in place of the piano.

Another teacher plays the song in its entirety as the pupils watch the words. Then she asks them to hum as she plays. Next they whisper the words rhythmically as she plays. Occasionally she stops and checks to see if they are in the right place. Then the children sing as she plays. She varies the procedure by asking the children to clap or tap the underlying pulse, the strong beat, or the rhythmic pattern of the melody as she plays. (See pp. 20, 21.)

¶ USING THE PHONOGRAPH — The piano method can be used with the phonograph. Some teachers gradually decrease the volume of the phonograph as the children become more familiar with the song. (Starting a record with the volume low, then increasing it to the desired intensity avoids the abrupt start caused by setting the needle down when the volume is up.)

All children enjoy occasionally learning a song from a recording. However, the teacher who can sing should not rely entirely upon the recordings. Nothing replaces the personality of the singer.

Singing a Song

¶ STARTING A SONG — Some classroom teachers start songs spontaneously whenever they feel that singing is appropriate or when a song fits into the other activities. This is natural and fine *if* the teacher has a good sense of pitch and can start the song in a key suitable for the group.

Songs may also be started by sounding the keynote, then the initial note. Some teachers use a pitch pipe. (The round chromatic type is best.) Others use various instruments. (See p. 60.) Some play a short introduction on the piano, then signal the starting time by a nod of the head. Others strum two or four measures on the autoharp or the ukelele and signal when the class is to begin.

Singing the first phrase of the song, then starting over again without losing a beat is a good way to start a song. The children know that they are expected to join the teacher when she starts the phrase the second time.

More formal methods of starting a song include conducting (see p. 22), and counting a measure to set the tempo. The teacher may say in rhythm, "One, two, ready, sing," if the song swings in two's and starts on the first beat of the measure. If the song swings in three's she would say, "One, two, three, one, ready, sing"; in four's,

"One, two, ready, sing." If the song swings in four's and starts on the fourth beat, she would say, "One, ready, sing."

¶ MEANS OF SONG ENRICHMENT — Songs may be enriched by adding rhythmic activities suitable to the song, by dramatization, by use of instruments as accompaniments or as sound effects (See Chapters II and III), or by use of finger plays. (See p. 97.) Traditional rhythmic activities are suitable at times, especially in singing games, but the use of suggestions which have been made by the children for enriching the song encourages interest, discrimination, and good thinking.

¶ PHRASING (See pp. 23-26 and 49, 50) — Phrase recognition should not be considered an activity for primary children only. It should be continued throughout the elementary school and into the junior and senior high schools. Breathing at the ends of phrases rather than in the middle makes the song more intelligible and more beautiful. Recognition of like phrases saves time in reading new songs.

¶ SINGING GAMES — The young child learns singing games by playing them over and over. Often the words tell the child the

A singing game,
"Bean Porridge Hot"

actions to be used. Directions for games should be simple. Children may also be encouraged to think of original actions.

Unless recordings are being used, it is wise to divide the class into two parts for the more vigorous games. One section may be the choir while the other plays the game. Then the pupils trade parts so that all have the opportunity to do both the singing and the action. This procedure keeps the song moving and prevents the singers from being out of breath. Too often singing games result in action for the children with the teacher doing the singing. On the other hand, it is claimed that some children find their singing voices while moving.

Development of a Permanent Repertoire

The school music program should give every child a repertoire of songs that will fulfill the needs of his life both in and out of school. This should include songs to sing for fun, patriotic songs, hymns, and folk songs. Development of a permanent repertoire may be begun in the kindergarten. The following cumulative song repertoire may serve as a guide. The grade levels are not arbitrary, but merely *suggested*. Many songs from the upper level will be enjoyed by the lower levels, and some of the songs for the lower levels will be enjoyed by the intermediate and upper levels. The teacher should be guided by the interests of the children. These songs are part of our heritage, but seem to be fast slipping away from us.

Grade levels *Sources°*

Kindergarten-Primary

A-hunting We Will Go	3:42 23:46 34:42 45:39
America	3:93 5:23 8:186 9:202 13:70 20:66 23:151 24:106 26:1 29:199 30:226 34:87 39:86 44:148 45:211 46:125
America, the Beautiful	1:170 9:200 13:86 14:211 15:143 20:65 23:149 24:107 29:35 34:147 39:90 45:209 46:126
Away in a Manger	3:226 14:64 20:78 23:125 25:16 31:119 34:80 39:80 46:29
Baa, Baa, Black Sheep	3:250 23:27 26:109 33:155
Battle Hymn of the Republic (cho.)	3:94 7:64 33:107 34:87 39:87 45:210
Columbia, the Gem of the Ocean (cho.)	3:94 7:64
Did You Ever See a Lassie?	3:9 13:143 17:41 26:54 45:33
Eency Weency Spider	33:159 39:9 42:126

Singing around the Christmas tree

	39:86 40:96 41:126 44:148 45:211 46:125
America, the Beautiful	1:170 4:189 9:200 10:198 13:86 14:211 15:143 23:149 27:1 30:35 37:154 40:95 44:147 46:126
Are You Sleeping? (round)	6:51 10:40 20:11 37:33 39:51 45:137
Auld Lang Syne	6:62 10:112 14:219 37:29 45:175
Blow the Man Down	10:117 14:173 37:76 44:27 45:150
Brahms' Lullaby	2:62 10:90 13:11 15:26 23:58 41:77 45:144
Bridge of Avignon, The	10:41 21:46 27:72 36:53
Come, Thou Almighty King	11:84 14:233 15:140 29:75 36:74 40:73 41:12
Come, Ye Thankful People, Come	2:177 14:236 27:39 28:48 29:46
Deck the Hall	13:36 32:169 36:102 38:162 44:114 45:196
Easter Parade, The	Sheet music
First Noel, The	15:130 23:126 28:59 30:59 30:71 33:95 37:135 38:130 40:39 44:120 45:198
God Bless America!	Sheet music
Goodby, Old Paint	10:142 15:123 16:148 32:46 36:46
Hark, the Herald Angels	38:155 40:91 41:118 45:194
Home on the Range	14:217 15:120 16:148 21:29 23:95 32:48 36:10 37:11 40:38 44:30 45:126
Hush, Little Baby	36:64 42:147
It Came Upon a Midnight Clear	23:127 36:102 37:134
Jingle Bells	14:226 23:120 24:69 28:79 36:140 44:111
Joy to the World	2:180 15:128 30:70 37:151
Little Sandman, The (Dustman)	6:65 10:181 19:39 32:151 36:65 44:108 45:80
Lovely Evening (round)	2:61 19:6 23:56 29:193 32:143 36:121 44:128
Now the Day Is Over	23:137 44:73
O Dear, What Can the Matter Be?	10:196 23:94 32:60 44:49
Old Brass Wagon	2:105 10:64 14:128 24:64
Old Folks at Home	1:30 9:14 13:8 15:58 30:180 40:65 41:70 44:20 45:191 46:33
Old MacDonald Had a Farm	23:96 36:14 40:136
O Little Town of Bethlehem	23:122 28:53 33:93 34:79 38:156
O Susanna	6:5 10:66 13:117 15:54 24:110
Paw-Paw Patch, The	9:54 13:140 22:116 24:27 28:2 36:50 45:75
Pop Goes the Weasel	1:166 7:130 13:82 23:70 27:108 32:38 36:50 45:56
Praise God from Whom All Blessings	

Upper Grades

God of Our Fathers	4:104 14:233
God Rest Ye Merry, Gentlemen	30:78
I Got Shoes (Robe, Crown)	2:102 22:16 44:86
I've Been Workin' on the Railroad	16:152 22:86 32:123 36:35 38:7 44:133
Jacob's Ladder	11:142 14:228 16:134 41:83 44:89 45:177 46:16
La Cucaracha	2:149 44:40
Liza Jane	32:140 36:79 41:15 44:25
Marine's Hymn, The	2:10 13:76 14:209 24:116 29:60 41:129 45:216
Merry Life, A	44:60
Mighty Fortress Is Our God, A	38:144
My Bonnie	13:36 37:69
My Old Kentucky Home	1:167 37:91 45:190
Now Thank We All Our God	2:176 41:108 44:73
O God, beneath Thy Guiding Hand	4:105 14:235 30:11 37:105
O My Darling Clementine	14:218 29:160 37:67 38:84 44:132
O Sole Mio	37:52
Over the Rainbow	Sheet music
O Worship the King	16:139 30:123 37:100
Polly-Wolly-Doodle	2:12 14:225 28:8 36:8 38:14 40:56
Red River Valley	16:34 37:58 44:32 46:5
Reuben and Rachel	4:57 11:192 14:223 37:45
Shenandoah	4:115 14:27 15:97 37:76 44:26 46:12
Stars of the Summer Night	2:206 14:27 15:84
Star-Spangled Banner, The	4:190 6:186 11:198 14:216 15:142 28:1 30:222 32:176 36:110 37:153 38:133 41:124 44:149 45:214 46:124
Stodola Pumpa (Walking at Night)	14:136 16:91 19:19 37:9 41:21 44:43 46:56
Sweet and Low	1:29 11:12 14:213 27:139 36:68 45:185
Swing Low, Sweet Chariot	14:229 37:118 40:74 44:82 45:181
That's an Irish Lullaby	Sheet music
Way up on Old Smoky	38:37
When Johnny Comes Marching Home	16:25 23:152 29:20 37:160
White Christmas	Sheet music
Winter Wonderland	Sheet music
Yankee Doodle	9:46 13:74 14:220 16:18 21:48 23:148 40:12

Most of these songs may also be found in the new series now in press.

° Refer to Bibliography, pp. 112, 113. In each case, the first number given here refers to the number of the book as listed in the Bibliography; the second number, to the page in that book.

¶ FINGER PLAYS — Finger plays are fun for young children. They like to follow the action and join in the rhyme. In combining music with finger plays, the child is given a chance for enjoyable participation. Every child takes part, all hands are occupied, and tension is eased as the fingers follow the action of the song. Children should be encouraged to create their own words and action. Finger plays are also desirable for quieting and relaxing an active group. This quiet period may well follow the more strenuous play period or precede the rest period. Example:

Knock at the Door
(*Our First Music*, 3:31)

Words	*Finger action*
Knock at the door,	Tap on forehead
Peep in,	Lift eyelid
Lift the latch	Pull up on end of nose
And walk in	Point to open mouth

(Actions are merely suggestions; children should think up their own actions.)
Other examples include:

American Singer, I
  Dance, Thumbkin, Dance   (7:99)

The Kindergarten Book
  Here Is the Beehive   (34:37)
  Five Little Chickadees   (34:37)
  Finger Game   (34:51)
  Where Is Thumbkin?   (34:51)

Music Through the Day
  Five Black Horses   (31:52)
  Three Blue Pigeons   (31:101)

Musical literacy —
a need for our children

Music Reading

Music reading is a controversial topic among educators. At one time music reading was the main objective of music in the elementary schools. Songs were chosen largely because they were considered easy to read, or because they contained figures designed to simplify reading problems. Songs were composed for the purpose of teaching note-reading. A good song springs from the heart. It comes from the people. It expresses something that cries for expression. Songs written to teach a problem are seldom interesting or beautiful. If the problem cannot be found in a really musical song, why teach the problem song?

Today, music reading is the outcome of genuine musical experiences. Some of the musical experiences already described which contribute to music reading include:

Recognition of walking, running, and skipping rhythms
Response to long notes
Response to the accent
Recognition of like and unlike phrases
Ability to read and write line notation

Ability to change line notation to standard notation
Understanding of measure signatures
Understanding of the measure bars
Understanding of note and rest values
Ability to play simple tunes on the melody bells
Ability to play simple melodies and chords on the piano
Ability to play the autoharp, recognizing chord changes
Ability to play the ukelele
Ability to play the tonette or similar instrument
Knowledge of the staff
Use of the singing voice

Music reading comes from experience. If the children sing many songs with the guidance of the teacher when they need it, they will gradually become more independent.

Different teachers use different techniques. Some use the numbers 1 to 8, some the letters A to G, some the syllables do-re-mi-fa-so-la-ti-do, and many use position on the staff. At present writing there seems to be a trend toward the latter.

Some start with the chant

Practically every child can chant. (This is also a good starting point for children to find their singing voices.) Newsboys use it in selling papers. Children use it constantly in play. They use it in teasing. Who has not heard, "John has a girl friend" sung on these notes?

There are a number of songs built on the chant. Most of the book, *Singing as We Play* (35), is based on the chant. Other examples include:

New Music Horizons, Bk. II
Busy People   (26:83)

Singing on Our Way
Here Is the Beehive   (39:43)

Songs Children Sing
Itiskit, Itaskit   (23:11)

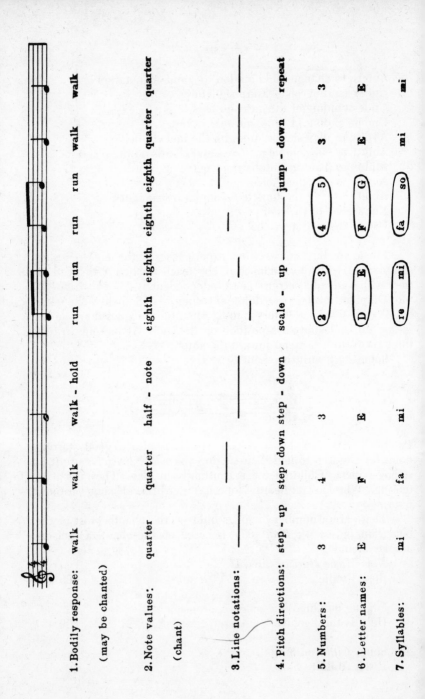

1. Bodily response: (may be chanted)	walk	walk	walk - hold	run run run run	run run	walk	walk
2. Note values: (chant)	quarter	quarter	half - note	eighth eighth eighth eighth	eighth eighth	quarter	quarter
3. Line notations:	—	—	—	— — —	— —	—	—
4. Pitch directions:	step - up	step - down	step - down	scale - up	jump - down	repeat	
5. Numbers:	3	4	3	2 3	4 5	3	3
6. Letter names:	E	F	E	D E	F G	E	E
7. Syllables:	mi	fa	mi	re mi	fa so	mi	mi

Other teachers ask the children to use their hands to show the pitch direction up or down. Children observe whether the notes step scalewise up, step scalewise down, repeat, jump up or jump down. (The terms "step" and "jump" may confuse the child accustomed to bodily activity.)

The phrase on the opposite page illustrates several different techniques.

In the number system, the keynote is *1*. When using the syllables in the movable *do* system, the keynote is *do*. (When the stationary *do* is used, middle C is always *do*.)

Some teachers use "tonal patterns." That is, the children learn a rote song containing a tonal pattern such as *do-mi-so* or 1-3-5. Then they learn the syllables or numbers of the tonal pattern. They locate familiar tonal patterns in new songs. Gradually they build a vocabulary of tonal patterns which they recognize and sing in new songs. Eventually they sight-read entire songs. Most texts and teachers' manuals suggest suitable tonal patterns.

The interval method uses definite songs to represent intervals. For example, "My bon-" from *My Bonnie* is a major sixth. Whenever the children see a major sixth they recall how it should sound by association with the first two notes of *My Bonnie*. Other songs are used for other intervals.

When asked by her successor what method she had used in teaching the children to read so well, one teacher replied that she had not taught music reading. Then she mentioned that she had taught the class to play tonettes! Most persons who play instruments can read vocally, *if* they have been taught to *think pitch* rather than merely to finger the notes.

Thinking is essential in reading music. Analysis of the song simplifies reading. If the class observes the phrases with like melodies or rhythmic patterns, much time is saved. If they recognize that they have already read the melody of a phrase, the students should observe the new words and sing it immediately. Time is also saved by recognition of *similarity* in phrases. Suppose the second phrase is exactly like the first except that it is pitched a note or two higher or lower. Why read syllables, numbers or letters? Why not locate the initial pitch and proceed at once with the words? Or suppose that two phrases are identical with the exception of the endings. It should be necessary to *read* only the endings, then sing the whole phrase with the words. If there is a scale passage in a song, children should be taught to look at the first and the last notes and to move quickly up or down the scale between the notes. It is neither necessary nor advisable to read each note individually. Repeated notes should be grasped quickly rather than read individually.

Part Singing

¶ HARMONY-READINESS — Children in the primary grades have had experience hearing harmony. They have heard autoharp, ukelele and piano accompaniments. Perhaps their teachers occasionally sang descants or other harmony parts while the children sang the melody.

When children can sing the melody well and have had some of the foregoing experiences in harmony, they are ready for part singing. Most fifth grades and some fourth grades are ready for this experience. At this age children enjoy working in groups. Often children in the primary grades can sing simple harmony.

¶ HARMONIZATION "BY EAR" — Some children are able to harmonize by ear. Others can learn to do so. One way to introduce harmonization is by use of the autoharp. Children pick tones from the tonic or I chord of a familiar song, then change as other chords are sounded throughout the song. *Down in the Valley* (2:26) and *Doney Gal* (29:102) are excellent songs for initial experiences in this type of activity.

Another procedure is singing in thirds. A familiar song such as *For He's a Jolly Good Fellow* (29:153) or *Billy Boy* (13:80) is good for the first trial. All of the pupils sing it in unison. Then part of the class sings the melody, while the others, with some help, follow the melody a third lower. That is, if *Billy Boy* starts on G, the harmony part will start on E♭ below. There may be spots in the song where thirds will not sound pleasing. Children will automatically make the necessary adjustments "by ear." After a few attempts by the more adventurous members, the class may be divided, one half singing the melody and the other, the harmony. When the one group becomes accustomed to harmonizing, the other group should have an opportunity to try it, in order that all the children may have the fun of singing a harmony part.

A number of teachers have been more successful in starting harmonization by selecting songs which are harmonized a third *higher* than the melody. *Merrily We Roll Along* may be harmonized in this manner.

Some songs suitable for harmonization by ear include:

That's an Irish Lullaby (Chorus)	Sheet music
The Whiffenpoof Song (Chorus)	Sheet music

From *New Music Horizons*, V
    The Old Mexican Woman   (29:71)

From *Our Land of Song*
    Covered Wagon Days   (4:5)

From *American Singer*, V
    Singing Together
    Jacob's Ladder   (11:142, 41:83)
    The Prairie Schooner   (11:51)

The fifth book of each of the five basic series is full of excellent material for this activity. Some of the songs can be harmonized by using both thirds and sixths. *Silent Night, Shoo Fly,* and *Stodola Pumpa* are good examples.

Children should be encouraged to form small groups to sing "barber-shop harmony." This activity appeals strongly to boys of the fifth and sixth grades.

Harmonizing by ear should first be experienced *without* seeing the music. This forces the children to rely entirely upon their hearing. Later they will discover in their books that thirds *look alike*, that is, if a note is on a line, the third above or the third below is also on a line. If it is in a space, the other note is also in a space. Pupils will also find that sixths do *not* look alike. If one note is on a line, the other is in a space, and vice versa. These discoveries, together with the ability to hear thirds and sixths, will make the reading of parts much easier. When children know the melody of a song, they should be able to read the harmony part. The occasional fourths, fifths, seconds, and sevenths will fall in naturally between the thirds and sixths.

¶ CHORDING (See p. 64) — Vocal chording will help establish a feeling for harmony. The class sings a familiar song such as *Our Boys Will Shine Tonight, La Cucaracha* (chorus) or *Skip to My Lou*. As the class sings, they clap the strong beats. Then part of the class sings the melody while the others sing *do* or *I* on the strong beats. Pupils listen to discover unpleasant harmonies, and change to *so* or V when necessary. Songs requiring only the I and V chords, such as *Down in the Valley* and *Polly-Wolly-Doodle,* are best for initial experiences in chording. The words of the song may be written on the board and the chord changes indicated below the words. (See p. 64.) The song may then be transferred to a card for future reference. Then the class sings the song with the words, part of the children singing the melody, and the others singing the harmony. Pupils may also play the chords on the autoharp, the ukelele, or the piano. Some songs require the use of *fa* or *IV. Silent Night* is a good example. The chords in this song correspond to the bass part. Chording creates a good third part in some cases. For example, a class sings *Silent Night* in two parts using thirds and sixths, then adds the roots or basic tones of the chords as the third part. Although *Silent Night* is easy to harmonize, it is frequently sung out of tune. Teachers should encourage children to be especially alert to intonation when singing this song (see p. 106 for helps on intonation). Some good songs for early experiences in chording include:

American Singer, Bk. V	(11:27)
New Music Horizons, Bk. V	(29:157)
We Sing	(6:92)
Shoo Fly	
Music Everywhere	(2:12)
New Music Horizons, Bk. IV	(28:8)
Singing on Our Way	(39:8)
Polly-Wolly-Doodle	
New Music Horizons, Bk. V	(29:160)
O My Darling Clementine	
Music Everywhere	(2:26)
Music Near and Far	(32:69)
Down in the Valley	

¶ ROUNDS — Rounds such as *Row, Row, Row Your Boat* and *Three Blind Mice* are good for recreational singing. They encourage independence rather than harmony, however. Who has not seen a child holding his fingers in his ears in order that he may not hear the other parts? If children are not taught to keep the rhythm flowing and to listen to each other as they sing rounds, they may develop habits of poor intonation. It is also fun to clap, step or play rounds on rhythm instruments. Children enjoy dramatizing *Three Blind Mice* as a round.

¶ CANONS — A round is the simplest form of canon. However, in a canon the second or third part need not be exactly like the first. Generally the parts end simultaneously. Examples include:

American Singer, Bk V The First Tulip	(11:144)
Music Everywhere New Year's Carol	(2:182)
New Music Horizons, Bk. V Thankful Song	(29:125)
Our Land of Song Reuben and Rachel	(4:57)
Singing Together Goin' to Leave Ol' Texas	(41:58)

¶ DESCANTS — A descant is a melody composed to harmonize with another melody. Descants are fun to sing, but, like rounds, are often sung out of tune. Descants created by the children seem to avoid this tendency, because the children must listen while creating them. Excerpts of songs may be repeated on different pitches to harmonize with the melody. For example, "Swing low" can be repeated over and over to harmonize with the melody in *Swing Low, Sweet Chariot* (44:82).

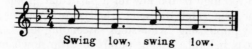

Another part is easily made by singing the above descant a third higher.

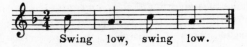

Swing   low,   swing   low.

The root and the fifth of the chord may be used to make another descant.

Swing low,   Swing low.

The above descants may be used separately, or all may be used simultaneously, making four parts in all.

¶ IMPROVEMENT OF INTONATION AND TONE QUALITY — Music is an art. If it is not an aesthetic experience, it has missed the mark. Children *can* sing artistically. They can keep the melody flowing. They can interpret the mood and the meaning of the song. Good interpretation alone will solve many problems. It will make the music more enjoyable. It will improve the tone quality. If the *children themselves* decide how the song should be interpreted, they will remember how to sing it, and will enjoy carrying out their own ideas. Good interpretation will also improve the intonation. (Intonation means singing or playing in tune, neither too low [flat], nor too high [sharp].)

Children are more likely to flat than to sharp. Good posture reduces flatting and is necessary for breath control. A room well-ventilated and not too hot contributes to good intonation. A happy room atmosphere improves both intonation and tone quality. Keeping the song up to tempo improves intonation. (Children are inclined to drag the tempo if not reminded occasionally.) Varying the tempo from time to time keeps the children alert. Some songs are written too high or too low for a particular group. If the class sings out of tune, pitch the song a half step higher or lower. Suggesting that pupils sing "wide steps" ascending and "narrow steps" descending is helpful. Asking pupils to drop down on their high tones like landing jet planes, or as if they were climbing ladders and placing their feet from *above* the rungs rather than even with the rungs, are good techniques.

The teacher should keep her own tone light and free. She can occasionally check the pitch of the song by using the pitch pipe or other instrument. She should avoid overdoing this procedure. Children should become conscious of pitch, but the spontaneity of singing should not be continually interrupted by checking errors. Spontaneity itself will contribute to good tone quality and intonation.

¶ SOME SUGGESTIONS FOR PART SINGING — It is important that some independent singers be seated in each section. It is also important that each section has an opportunity to sing the melody on some songs, and harmony on others. Too often the better singers are assigned to the second or third part because they find it easy. Many adults claim to have lost their high tones through this procedure. This is unfortunate because these are the people who will sing throughout their lives and will need their complete ranges. Until the voices start changing, a singing section should sing the melody on two or three songs, then the harmony on the next two or three songs. The teacher should indicate in her song book the group singing the melody on each song. In this way she avoids confusion and arguments. Teachers have tried having both groups learn both parts to each song, but often this procedure results in neither part being well learned. The whole class feels insecure and confused.

When a few voices have become too low to sing high comfortably, these students may be seated in the center of the class. Without changing seats they can then sing with the group singing the lower part. Use of the terms Part I, Part II, and Part III in place of soprano, second soprano, and alto has its advantages. Some boys feel that the term "soprano" is sissy. Some mothers object to their daughters singing "alto." When a boy frowns and seems to strain for his high tones, it is a good indication that it is time to place him on a lower part.

If the classroom teacher is unable to carry a harmony part herself, she can help students by playing the piano or another instrument. If she can neither sing nor play, part singing will necessarily be restricted to harmonization by students who are able to sing parts unassisted.

Part singing should *never* become a laborious chore in which the children are required to work out their parts, note by note.

The Changing Voice

Occasionally in the fifth grade, but more often in the sixth, some of the voices begin to assume a richer, fuller tone quality. This is especially true of the boys. Some of the boys, just before the change, will develop a beautiful, brilliant tone quality and a very high range. With very little effort some of them can sing to C above the treble staff. Most of these boys love to sing.

Then they begin to develop a sort of huskiness. Some of them say they "have a cold." This is a fair indication that their voices are beginning to change. They will lose their high tones. Some of their voices go down in pitch gradually, while others drop very low in the bass clef range, almost overnight. (Some of these low voices will gradually become higher later. Some will eventually become tenors.) The first group should be placed on the second part (alto) until even this is too high, then on the third (alto-tenor) part, and finally on the fourth (bass). If only one voice in the class is low enough for bass (unless he can carry a part independently), he may be placed with whichever group is singing an octave above his range; then he sings the notes an octave lower. This is where the male elementary teacher can be particularly helpful. He can sing with the boy to give him a feeling of security. A woman should play the part on the piano in the bass clef.

Boys approach the change with varied feelings about their voices. Some feel that it is manly to sing low, and they may pretend that their voices have gone down before they actually have, especially if their best friends have moved to the lower part. Others do not want to give up singing soprano. Some of the attachment to the soprano part may be due to the fact that the soprano often carries the melody. For this reason it is important that each part has opportunities to sing the melody while other parts sing the harmony.

This is a fine time for the study of stringed instruments. The thicker, lower strings can be compared to the thickening vocal chords. If some member of the class plays a 'cello or other bass instrument, he may be encouraged to play the part with the new bass singers.

The voices of some of the girls may change somewhat, but a true contralto seldom appears in the elementary school.

When the first voice changes, the opportune time to study voice classification has arrived. Children should hear records of good adult voices singing selections which the children will enjoy and understand. Most opera arias do not appeal to children in the elementary school. Coloratura sopranos usually draw giggles rather than appreciation from children.

Approximate ranges of the children's voices during the sixth to the ninth grades are

(The whole notes indicate the range of the majority of the children. The black dots indicate possible ranges.)

Reading Part Songs

The experiences in harmonizing by ear, singing rounds and descants should make the reading of parts much easier. In starting the song, the keynote and the initial note of each part should be

Singing to autoharp accompaniment

sounded on the pitch pipe, the bells, or the piano. After more experience children can get their tones from a chord. Each group may hold its initial tone softly for a few seconds, then start at a given signal from the teacher.

In addition to observing like and similar phrases, scales, patterns, and repeated notes (see pp. 98, 99), children should become accustomed to looking for thirds, sixths and the basic tones of the chords in the harmony. Many three-part songs are written mostly in these simple harmonies which the children have already been singing by ear. The melody should be located, as it appears in the different parts. Canonical effects should be observed (see p. 105).

One teacher teaches the melody of the song first, then after analysis of harmonic effects, such as thirds and sixths, adds the other parts. If a section has difficulty, she sings the words with that part as the other sections hum their parts. This keeps all students working while the one part is being guided.

The class should be encouraged to try to read all parts simultaneously. Learning each part as a separate melody tends to increase independence at the expense of the development of aural powers. Idle sections may become restless while awaiting their turn for drill.

A teacher should not insist upon laborious note reading to the extent that the children dislike the song before they have learned to sing it. Insight and guided experience in singing many beautiful and interesting songs increase reading power more than intense drill upon a few dull songs written with so-called *easy* interval progressions.

Questions for Class Discussion

UNISON SINGING
1. Characterize the new conception of the voice of the primary child.
2. What classifications of singers in the primary grades are recommended? Describe each.
3. What seating arrangements are recommended? Which do you favor, and why?
4. List the criteria for songs suitable for children.
5. What is a "rote song"? Should the children who have difficulty in singing be allowed to sing with the independent singers when a new rote song is being learned?
6. Give as many suggestions as possible for helping children learn to carry a tune.
7. Describe four different ways to teach a rote song. When would you use each?
8. Discuss the use of the piano (or other instrument) as an accompaniment to singing.

9. What factors of artistic singing can be accomplished by children in the elementary school?
10. What is meant by *intonation?* How can intonation be improved?
11. Discuss the importance of individual singing.
12. How would you start a song? Be explicit.

PART SINGING

1. When is part singing generally begun? When would you say a class may profitably engage in part singing?
2. Should part singing be introduced aurally or visually? Justify your answer.
3. What harmonic experiences may be furnished children before they begin part singing?
4. What *beginning* experiences in part singing are suitable for children, and why?
5. How should the pupils of a class be seated or divided for part singing? Should they always sing the same parts? Why, or why not?
6. Characterize the changing voice.
7. Keeping in mind the psychology of adolescence, how would you help a boy whose voice is changing?
8. What is a descant? a round? a canon?
9. How would you go about teaching children to chord vocally?
10. Give the approximate ranges for: Soprano, alto, alto-tenor and bass voices as you would find them in the upper grades.

MUSIC READING

1. In what way would the following musical activities prepare children to read music:
   A. Responses to natural rhythms
   B. Recognition of phrases, like and unlike
   C. Response to notes longer than walking notes
   D. Response to accents
   E. Writing line notation
   F. Use of instruments
   G. Recognition of high and low pitch
2. What three means of tonal identification are used in our schools today? Which predominates? Which do you prefer, and why?
3. What are the advantages and the disadvantages of reading by staff distance only?
4. What principles underlie the use of drill activities in teaching elementary children music?
5. Familiarize yourself with the teacher's manuals of the current school music series and compare them.

Bibliography

1. Armitage, Theresa et al, *Merry Music*. Boston: C. C. Birchard & Co., 1939, 1953.

2. Armitage, Theresa et al, *Music Everywhere*. Boston: C. C. Birchard & Co., 1943, 1955.

3. Armitage, Theresa et al, *Our First Music*. Boston: C. C. Birchard & Co., 1941.

4. Armitage, Theresa et al, *Our Land of Song*. Boston: C. C. Birchard & Co., 1942, 1956.

5. Armitage, Theresa et al, *Our Songs*. Boston: C. C. Birchard & Co., 1939, 1952.

6. Armitage, Theresa et al, *We Sing*. Boston: C. C. Birchard & Co., 1940, 1953.

7. Beattie, John W. et al, *American Singer*, Bk. I. New York: American Book Co., 1954.

8. Beattie, John W., et al, *American Singer*, Bk. II. New York: American Book Co., 1954.

9. Beattie, John W. et al, *American Singer*, Bk. III. New York: American Book Co., 1954.

10. Beattie, John W. et al, *American Singer*, Bk. IV. New York: American Book Co., 1954.

11. Beattie, John W. et al, *American Singer*, Bk. V. New York: American Book Co., 1955.

12. Brody, Viola, "The Role of Body Awareness in the Emergence of Musical Ability; Its Application to Music Education, the College Basic Music Course and Critic Teaching," *Journal of Research in Music Education*, Vol. 1, Fall, 1954, pp. 21-24.

13. Dykema, Peter W. et al, *Happy Singing*. Boston: C. C. Birchard & Co., 1947.

14. Dykema, Peter W. et al, *Music in the Air*. Boston: C. C. Birchard & Co., 1947.

15. Dykema, Peter W. et al, *Sing!* Boston: C. C. Birchard & Co., 1953.

16. Dykema, Peter W. et al, *Sing Out!* Boston: C. C. Birchard & Co., 1946.

17. Guessford, Margaret and Hamlin, Alice, *Singing Games*. Cincinnati: Willis Music Co., 1941.

18. Jersild, Arthur T. and Bienstock, Sylvia, "A Study of the Development of Children's Ability to Sing," *Journal of Educational Psychology*, XXV, Oct., 1934, 481-503.

19. Krone, Beatrice A. and Max, *Our First Songs to Sing with Descants*. Chicago: Neil A. Kjos Music Co., 1941, 1949.

20. Krone, Max et al, *Music 'round the Clock*. Chicago: Follett Pub. Co., 1955.

21. Krone, Max et al, *Music Round the Town*. Chicago: Follett Pub. Co., 1955.

22. Landeck, Beatrice, *Songs to Grow On*. New York: Edward B. Marks Music Corp., 1950.

23. Martin, Florence and White, Margaret Rose, ed. & arr., *Songs Children Sing*. Chicago: Hall & McCreary Co., 1935, 1942.

24. McConathy, Osbourne et al, *Music for Early Childhood*. New York: Silver Burdett Co., 1952.

25. McConathy, Osbourne et al, *New Music Horizons*, Bk. 1. New York: Silver Burdett Co., 1944.

26. McConathy, Osbourne et al. *New Music Horizons*, Bk. II. New York: Silver Burdett Co., 1944.

27. McConathy, Osbourne et al, *New Music Horizons*, Bk. III. New York: Silver Burdett Co., 1944.

28. McConathy, Osbourne et al, *New Music Horizons*, Bk. IV. New York: Silver Burdett Co., 1945.

29. McConathy, Osbourne et al, *New Music Horizons*, Bk. V. New York: Silver Burdett Co., 1946.

30. McConathy, Osbourne et al, *New Music Horizons*, Bk. VI. New York: Silver Burdett Co., 1946.

31. Mursell, James L. et al, *Music Through the Day*. New York: Silver Burdett Co., 1956.

32. Mursell, James L. et al, *Music Near and Far*. New York: Silver Burdett Co., 1956.

33. Pitts, Lilla Belle et al, *The First Grade Book*. Boston: Ginn & Co., 1949.

34. Pitts, Lilla Belle et al, *The Kinder-*

garten Book. Boston: Ginn & Co., 1949.

35. Pitts, Lilla Belle et al, *Singing as We Play.* Boston: Ginn & Co., 1949.

36. Pitts, Lilla Belle et al, *Singing Every Day.* Boston: Ginn & Co., 1950.

37. Pitts, Lilla Belle et al, *Singing in Harmony.* Boston: Ginn & Co., 1951.

38. Pitts, Lilla Belle et al, *Singing Juniors.* Boston: Ginn & Co., 1954.

39. Pitts, Lilla Belle et al, *Singing on Our Way.* Boston: Ginn & Co., 1949.

40. Pitts, Lilla Belle et al, *Singing and Rhyming.* Boston: Ginn & Co., 1950.

41. Pitts, Lilla Belle et al, *Singing Together.* Boston: Ginn & Co., 1951.

42. Seeger, Ruth Crawford, *American Folk Songs for Children.* Garden City, N. Y.: Doubleday & Co., Inc. 1948.

43. Sheehy, Emma Dickson, *There's Music in Children.* New York: Henry Holt & Co., Inc., revised 1952.

44. Wilson, Harry and Frey, Hugo, arr., *Sing Along.* New York: J. J. Robbins and Sons, 1948.

45. Wolfe, Irving et al, *Together We Sing.* Chicago: Follett Publishing Co., 1950.

46. Zanzig, Augustus D., compiler, *Singing America.* Boston: C. C. Birchard & Co., 1940.

Suggested Supplementary Song Sources

Association for Childhood Education, International, *Songs Children Like.* Washington, D. C.: ACE, 1954.

Bailey, Charity and Abeson, Marion, *Playtime with Music.* New York: Liveright Publishing Corp., 1952.

Bailey, Charity and Holsaert, Eunice, *Sing a Song with Charity Bailey.* New York: Plymouth Music Co., 1955.

Boni, Margaret B., *Fireside Book of Folk Songs.* New York: Simon & Schuster, Inc., 1947.

*Carmer, Carl, *America Sings.* New York: Alfred A. Knopf, Inc., 1942.

Coleman, Satis, *The New Singing Time.* New York: John Day Co., Inc., 1950.

Coopersmith, Harry, *The Songs We Sing.* New York: United Synagogue Commission on Jewish Education, 1950.

Crowninshield, Ethel, *Songs and Stories about Animals.* Boston: Boston Music Co., 1947.

*Davison, Archibald T. et al, *Songs of Freedom.* New York: Houghton Mifflin Co., 1942.

Eisenstein, Judith Kaplan, *Gateway to Jewish Songs.* New York: Belerman's Jewish Book House, 1939.

Ives, Burl, *The Burl Ives Song Book.* New York: Ballantine Books, 1953.

Krone, Beatrice and Max, *Descants and Easy Basses.* Chicago: Neil A. Kjos Music Co., 1950.

Krone, Beatrice and Max, *Descants for Christmas.* Chicago: Neil A. Kjos Music Co., 1949.

Krone, Beatrice and Max, *From Descants to Trios.* Chicago: Neil A. Kjos Music Co., 1944.

Krone, Beatrice and Max, *Great Songs of Faith.* Chicago: Neil A. Kjos Music Co., 1944.

Krone, Beatrice and Max, *Intermediate Descants.* Chicago: Neil A. Kjos, 1954.

Krone, Beatrice and Max, *More Descants and Easy Basses.* Chicago: Neil A. Kjos Music Co., 1951.

Krone, Beatrice and Max, *Our Third Book of Descants.* Chicago: Neil A. Kjos Music Co., 1948.

Krone, Beatrice and Max, *Songs for Fun with Descants.* Chicago: Neil A. Kjos, 1956.

Krone, Beatrice and Max, *Songs to Sing with Descants.* Chicago: Neil A. Kjos Music Co., 1940.

Krone, Beatrice and Max, *Very Easy Descants.* Chicago: Neil A. Kjos Music Co., 1951.

Landeck, Beatrice, *More Songs to Grow On.* New York: William Sloane Associates, 1954.

Landeck, Beatrice, *Songs My True Love Sings.* New York: Edward B. Marks Music Corporation, 1946.

Lomax, John and Alan, *American Ballads and Folk Songs.* New York: The Macmillan Co., 1934.

Lomax, John and Alan, *Folk Song: U.S.A.* New York: Duell, Sloan and Pearce, 1947.

Lomax, John and Alan, *Our Singing*

Country. New York: The Macmillan Co., 1941.

*Luther, Frank, *Americans and Their Songs.* New York: Harper & Bros., 1942.

Niles, John Jacob, *Ballads, Carols and Tragic Legends from the Southern Appalachian Mountains.* New York: G. Schirmer, Inc., 1937.

Norton, June, *Sing and Be Happy.* New York: John Day Co., 1951.

Ritchie, Jean, *The Swapping Song Book.* New York: Oxford University Press, 1952.

Sandburg, Carl, *The American Songbag.* New York: Harcourt, Brace & Co., Inc., 1927, 1946.

Sandburg, Carl, *The New American Songbag.* New York: Broadcast Music, Inc., 1950.

Scott, Tom, *Folk Songs for Singing.* New York: Chas. H. Hansen Music Corp., 1948.

*Scott, Tom, *Sing of America.* New York: Thomas Y. Crowell Co., 1947.

Seeger, Ruth Crawford, *American Folk Songs for Christmas.* Garden City, N. Y.: Doubleday & Co., 1953.

Seeger, Ruth Crawford, *Animal Folk Songs for Children.* Garden City, N. Y.: Doubleday & Co., 1950.

Siegmeister, Elie, *Work and Sing.* New York: Edward B. Marks, 1944.

Siegmeister, Elie, and Downes, Olin, *A Treasury of American Song.* New York: Alfred A. Knopf, Inc., 1943.

Skip to My Lou, 155 E. 44th St., New York: Girl Scouts.

*Surrette, Thomas W., *Songs from Many Lands.* Boston: Houghton Mifflin Co., 1937.

*Trent-Johns, Altona, *Play Songs of the Deep South.* Washington, D. C.: Associated Publishers, 1944.

Wilson, Harry et al, *Music Americans Sing.* New York: Silver Burdett Co., 1948.

RECORDS OF FOLK SONGS

American Folk Songs for Children sung by Peter Seeger. Folkways.

Early American Ballads sung by John Jacob Niles. Boone-Tolliver.

Favorite Folk Songs sung by Susan Reed. Columbia.

Folk Songs and Ballads sung by Richard Dyer-Bennett. Decca.

Folk Songs of Many Lands sung by Martha Schaume. Vanguard.

Kentucky Mountain Songs, Vols. 1 and 2, sung by Jean Ritchie. Elektra.

More Playtime Songs sung by Charity Bailey. Young People's Records.

More Songs to Grow On sung by Alan Mills. Folkways.

Music Time sung by Charity Bailey. Folkways.

Obernnkirchen Children's Choir, Angel.

1, 2, 3 and a Zing Zing Zing, Folkways.

Play Party Songs sung by Leadbelly. Stinson.

Songs of Many Lands sung by Marais and Miranda. Decca.

Songs to Grow On sung by Woody Guthrie. Folkways.

Wayfaring Stranger sung by Burl Ives. Asch.

RECORDS FOR TEACHING SONGS TO CHILDREN

The American Singer Series, Beattie, John W. et al
    1 album for each grade, 1-8
    1 album for all grades combined

Music for Living Series, Mursell, James et al
    1 album (10 records) for each grade, 1-6

New Music Horizons Series, McConathy, Osbourne et al
    Music for Early Childhood album
    Series I: Songs from New Music Horizons, 6 albums, grades 1-6
    Series II: More Songs from New Music Horizons, 6 albums, grades 1-6
    Songs from World Music Horizons, Songs from American Music Horizons — 1 album for each book

Our Singing World Series, Pitts, Lilla Belle et al
    2 albums for each grade, Kindergarten-8
    Luthercords

Singing School Series, Armitage, Theresa et al
    1 album each, grades 1-8
    Happy Singing, grades 1-4 combined, Music in the Air, grades 1-8 combined, 1 album for each book

*out of print

Together We Sing Series, Wolfe, Irving et al
    2 albums for each book; 4 albums for *Together We Sing* (book for combined grades)

FILMS

Beginning Music Reading Experience, Los Angeles Public Schools, Sentous Center, 1205 W. Pico Blvd., Los Angeles, Calif.

Merry Christmas, Sterling 1949, 12 min. Vienna Choir Boys singing.
Pitchpipe, The, Johnson-Hunt Co. 10 min.
Search, The (for a folk song), University of Arkansas, Young America Films, Inc.
Two-Part Singing, Johnson-Hunt Co. 20 min.
Young America Sings. Units for grades 3, 4 and 5. Miessner, W. Otto et al, Young America Films, Inc.

Additional References

Adams, Fay, *Educating America's Children.* New York: Ronald Press, 1946, pp. 401-407.

Armitage, Theresa et al, *Teachers' Manuals I-VI*, Singing School Series. Boston: C. C. Birchard & Co., 1948.

Beattie, John W. et al, *Teachers' Guides I-VI*, American Singer Series. New York: American Book Co., 1947.

Dykema, Peter W. and Cundiff, Hannah M., *School Music Handbook.* Boston: C. C. Birchard & Co., 1955.

Flagg, Marion, *Musical Learning.* Boston: C. C. Birchard & Co., 1949, pp. 105-171.

Gehrkens, Karl W., *Music in the Grade Schools.* Boston: C. C. Birchard & Co., 1934, pp. 14-15.

Grant, Parks, *Music for Elementary Teachers.* New York: Appleton-Century-Crofts, Inc., 1951, Ch. IV, VI through XXII.

Hood, Marguerite and Schultz, Ernest J., *Learning Music Through Rhythm.* Boston: Ginn & Co., 1949, pp. 87-100, 109, 116-132, 146-173.

Jersild, Arthur T. and Bienstock, Sylvia, "The Influence of Training on Vocal Ability in Three-year Old Children," *Child Development II*, Dec. 1931, 272-291.

Krone, Beatrice Perham, *Music in the New School.* Chicago: Neil A. Kjos Music Co., revised 1947.

Krone, Beatrice and Max, *Music Participation in the Elementary School.* Chicago: Neil A. Kjos Music Co., 1950.

Landeck, Beatrice, *Children and Music.* New York: William Sloane Associates, 1952, pp. 50-73.

*LeBow, Mary and Perris, Arnold, *The Music Road* I and II. Boston: C. C. Birchard & Co., 1954, 1955.

Lee, J. Murray and Dorris May, *The Child and His Curriculum.* New York: Appleton-Century Crofts, Inc., 1950, pp. 599-602, 610.

Leonhard, Charles, *A Song Approach to Music Reading.* New York: Silver Burdett Co., 1953.

Mathews, Paul W., *You Can Teach Music.* New York: E. P. Dutton & Co., 1953, Ch. III, IV.

McConathy, Osbourne et al. *Teachers' Manuals*, Primary and Intermediate. New York: Silver Burdett Co., 1948.

Moorhead, Gladys and Pond, Donald, *Music of Young Children I: Chant*, Pillsbury Foundation Studies. Santa Barbara, Cal.: Pillsbury Foundation for the Advancement of Music Education, 1941.

Morgan, Hazel Nohavec, *Music in American Education.* Washington D.C.: Music Educators National Conference, 1955, Ch. V-IX.

Morgan, Hazel Nohavec and Russell V., *Music Education in Action.* Chicago: Neil A. Kjos Music Co., 1954.

Mursell, James L., *Education for Musical Growth.* Boston: Ginn & Co., 1948, pp. 272-276, 230, 12, 56, 61-62, 216-217, 240-246, 291.

Mursell, James L., *Music and the Classroom Teacher.* New York: Silver Burdett Co., 1951, Ch. VI.

Myers, Louise Kifer, *Teaching Children Music in the Elementary School.* New York: Prentice-Hall, Inc., 1956, Ch. III, VII.

*out of print

Nye, Robert E. and Bergethon, Bjornar, *Basic Music for Classroom Teachers.* New York: Prentice-Hall, Inc., 1954.

Pitts, Lilla Belle et al, *Guide and Teaching Suggestions,* Kindergarten-3 and 4-6, Our Singing World Series. Boston: Ginn & Co., 1950.

Rorke, Genevieve, *Choral Teaching at the Junior High School Level.* Chicago: Hall & McCreary Co., 1947.

Seeger, Ruth Crawford, *American Folk Songs for Children.* Garden City, N. Y.: Doubleday & Co., 1953, pp. 13-48.

We use our listening center

CHAPTER V

Let's Listen

Listening is an integral part of all music. Singing becomes beautiful through listening to tone, the melody line, the rhythm, and the meaning of the song. How much more meaningful rhythm becomes when the child can follow the rhythm of the music. It is no longer a matter of symmetry and muscular coordination only, but also a matter of communication and understanding. Music reading can be taught incidentally through listening. (See p. 131.) The use of instruments, and, in fact, all phases of music are interwoven and become a great whole through listening.

Listening is the phase of music common to everyone. People listen throughout their lives, whether they realize it or not. Some listen with their bodies, some with their emotions, others with their minds. The more avenues of listening explored, the more persons will be reached, and the more completely each is reached. Unless some unfortunate experience has closed these avenues, they are all open to every child. It is the business of the elementary teacher to lead the child to explore and to discover.

Passive Listening

Listening can be passive or active. Passive listening has become all too common since the advent of radio and television. It has its uses in the case of dinner background music and for therapeutic purposes which will not be discussed here.

One type of passive listening of value in the elementary school is quiet music during rest period. Kindergarten children are entitled to hear the best as they drop off to sleep. The music which children hear then will become familiar to them and will seem to be "old friends" when met later under more active circumstances.

Children should have some opportunities to listen quietly to music with no comments from the teacher. Some schools have listening clubs composed of students who choose their own programs. Many bring their own records to share with the group. The noon hour is a good time for these listening clubs to meet. A listening booth equipped with phonograph, headphones, and a collection of records provides opportunities for children to listen to their favorite recordings.

Some schools have tried soft music during the lunch hour. There are two schools of thought regarding this use of music. Some educators feel that children are more quiet and courteous during the hearing of soft music. Others feel that children develop poor listening habits under these circumstances.

Active Listening

Active listening will be discussed here because of its contribution to the musical growth and development of the child.

SOME SUGGESTIONS FOR THE TEACHER

¶ CHOICE OF MUSIC — It is of the utmost importance that the teacher himself should like the music that is to be played. There is a wealth of good listening material for elementary schools. *Music for Young Listeners,* The Crimson Book (4), The Green Book (5), and The Blue Book (3), by Lillian Baldwin, are excellent. Some of the material in *The Pilot* (11) and *The Mentor* (10) by William Hartshorn is suitable for children in the elementary school. All of these books give excellent teaching suggestions and contain the themes of the music suggested. The workbooks, *O Say Can You Hear?* Books 1, 2, and 3 (12) by Margueritte House are helpful. *The RCA Basic Elementary School Record Library* albums contain practical helps for the teacher.

¶ PREPARATION OF THE TEACHER — After the music is selected, the teacher must listen to it over and over until he knows it well. He should know the melody well enough to hum it. He should know the rhythm, the harmony, the form, the instrumentation, the dynamics, and the effects of pitch. He should know which of these constituents predominates.

Then he should do some research about the music and the composer. Although it is not necessary that he give the students a long history of the composer, it is desirable that the teacher know more than the students. Any facts pertaining to the specific composition to be played may be briefly relayed to the pupils *if such facts contribute to understanding the music.* Special music teachers would do well to review their notes on music history and literature, to reread their symphony program notes and to do some extra research in the library. Many general classroom teachers, also, have taken music appreciation courses, and in some cases are better prepared to teach music listening than some of the music specialists. Teachers seeking credits toward salary increases should consider enrolling in music appreciation courses in colleges. If there is a good music radio station in the vicinity, a great deal may be learned from listening to its programs. Such stations are usually FM stations. Following the themes in *A Dictionary of Musical Themes* by Barlow and Morgenstern (6) can make listening a fascinating hobby.

After the facts are assembled, the teacher should replay the music and connect the facts with the music. He should list all of the features of the music which convey the intent of the composer.

¶ OVERALL LESSON PLANNING (Example p. 133) — First of all, the teacher must select the specific learning outcomes. Children can accumulate factual information, they can further develop habits and skills, or, most important, they can develop attitudes, ideals and appreciations.

Secondly, the teacher must choose the activity by which the pupils will accomplish the outcomes selected. Will the pupils respond rhythmically, with instruments, by singing, or will they discuss the music? For what should they listen?

Then the teacher must decide what will be his role in stimulating, motivating, and directing pupil activities. What can he do which will cause the children to accomplish what he has decided they should accomplish? Materials and equipment must be at hand. Something is lost when a lesson is delayed while the teacher runs for chalk, scarves, or instruments. Only occasionally does an unforeseen situation call for material not immediately available. Then the teacher must be flexible enough to get the material quickly and go ahead.

¶ EVALUATION OF THE LESSON — At the conclusion of the lesson

Getting acquainted with instruments and singers

the teacher should ask himself what the pupils know that they did not know before. What skills have they which they did not have before the lesson? What definite growth in attitudes and appreciations occurred during the lesson? What did the teacher do that he had planned, and what did he do that he had not planned? Did the children get the point, or not? If not, why? Evaluation by the pupils themselves must not be overlooked. The teacher who keeps evaluations for future reference will improve his presentations. Last of all, the teacher must ask what he can do to follow up the lesson.

¶ LISTENING ATTITUDES — The listening attitude of the teacher himself sets the stage for the listening experience. No matter how many times the teacher has heard a good musical composition, he can always hear something new in it. Children are quick to catch attitudes and are inclined to believe that there must be something interesting in the music if the teacher is attentive. The teacher who turns on the phonograph and then settles down to grading papers or writing on the board is *not* a good example for his pupils.

¶ CONCERT MANNERS (See p. 185) — In this day of radio and television, people are accustomed to talking while music is being played. Our concert audiences constantly reflect this attitude. The wise teacher will lead the children to discuss concert manners, and will encourage them to draw up their own rules of courtesy while listening. He will wait until the class is quiet before starting the record, and will stop it for a moment if someone forgets. This stopping of the music may seem unfair to the attentive listeners, but it is generally not necessary more than once or twice if the music is interesting and the lesson is well presented.

The teacher also must conform to the rules drawn up by the class. If someone comes to the door, he will either stop the phonograph or step outside to talk.

Music That Children Like

Adults are inclined to classify music from simple to complex, by grade levels, or by periods in history. Children are not aware of the difficulties of performance or of analysis. Good music cuts across all grade levels. If the melody is singable, children like it. If the rhythm is vital and interesting, they like it. Beautiful tone appeals to children. Music suggestive of a mood entrances some.

Descriptive or program music captures the interest of others.

Variety is important. Through variety in the music itself or in the approach, more children may be reached. Some like to move to the rhythm. Some are transported to another world of dreams. The intellectual approach reaches some. Even science may be the key.

¶ POPULAR MUSIC — Frequently the question of popular music arises. Some teachers in the junior and senior high schools have successfully begun a series of listening lessons by a brief study of the history of jazz, and have worked from that into other types of music. Although jazz appeals to many adults and adolescents, most children in the elementary school do not feel the need for studying it. Some children may be interested in knowing that Negro pianists developed ragtime by changing the steady beat of polkas, mazurkas, quadrilles, and other dances to a "ragged" or more syncopated rhythm. They may want to know about the funeral and the election bands of the Old South, the jug bands, the blues, and the "cutting contests." They may be surprised to learn that jazz is a manner of improvisation rather than a type of written composition.

The jazz movement started in New Orleans, and by means of river boats moved from New Orleans through Omaha and Kansas City to other river ports, then overland to Chicago and on to New York. There, under the direction of such people as Paul Whiteman and Duke Ellington, jazz bands started to develop a new sound, to enlarge, and to play from music written for them.

Styles of playing changed according to the players popular during a particular period. Beginning with the rags of the late 1800's, they progressed through blues, Dixieland, boogie-woogie, swing, "hot" jazz, be-bop, and "cool" jazz to progressive or experimental jazz.

Some music educators have tried to close their eyes and hope that jazz would go away, but it is still with us. It is a part of American living. The literature of jazz is rich, varied, and attractive to children. The judicious use of such material can help in teaching various phases of music, such as form and instrumentation, and it enables the teacher to show that jazz and other so-called popular music have their roots in music of the past. The records *Jazz Band* and *The Story of Jazz for Children*, together with *The First Book of Jazz* (13) are helpful and of interest to children in the elementary school.

It is sometimes fun to trace singing commercials and themes

A future Louis Armstrong?

of radio and television programs to folk songs and orchestral music.
Examples include:

"Pepsi-cola hits the spot,"
John Peel, English folk song

The FBI in Peace or War theme,
"March" from *The Love for Three Oranges* by Prokofiev

Dragnet theme,
The Unfinished Symphony, 1st movement, by Schubert

It is also interesting to trace some popular songs to their origins.

Examples include:

> "He's in Love" from *Kismet*
> "Polovtzian Dances" from *Prince Igor* by Borodin

> "Baubles, Bangles and Beads"; "The Sands of Time"; and "This
>   Is My Beloved" from *Kismet,*
> *String Quartet in D Major* by Borodin

Often the children will prefer the original settings of melodies to the
popular settings. At any rate, the schools owe it to the children to
give them some contact with music other than popular or jazz. The
ten per cent who may study music professionally will hear the other
music eventually, but the remaining ninety per cent may never know
how to listen to it if they do not become acquainted with it in school.

Some Suggested Approaches to Listening Activities

¶ RESPONSE TO RHYTHM — Shortly before Christmas, a primary
class, which was able to follow walking, running, and skipping music,
heard "March" from *The Nutcracker Suite* by Tchaikovsky. Without
telling the title of the music, the teacher asked the children to listen
to the music to see how it made them feel like moving. Then she
asked several to show what they felt. Several marched, one very
stiffly. When asked *why* he marched that way he replied, "Because
the music is stiff." The teacher played the music again, asking the
children to listen to see if they heard "stiff" music. After hearing
the record again, one little girl said, "It wasn't *all* stiff, some of it
was 'whirly'."

In this way the children discovered the two melodies in the
march and expressed it rhythmically. Soon the entire class was showing the difference between the two tunes, and one child suggested
that half of the class could be toy soldiers and half could be dancing
dolls. With a minimum of costuming this activity evolved into the
first grade contribution to the Christmas program.

A kindergarten group in another school used the same music
and interpreted it with jack-in-the-boxes and spinning tops. Large
cardboard cartons decorated by upper grade students with poster
paint were placed on the stage. A child was hidden in each. When
Melody (or Theme) A sounded, up popped the children wearing
conical paper caps. When Theme B sounded, they disappeared into

the cartons, and girls in full skirts were the tops spinning about between the jack-in-the-boxes.

It is not important for children to feel the music in accordance with the traditional written program notes for it. In some cases program notes were devised to appeal to the layman, and were added *after* the music was composed. The listening lesson should not become a guessing game, with only one *right* answer. Often, the ideas of the children are as good or better than the original notes. Teachers will get better response with "What, in the music, made you think that?" and "That shows good thinking," rather than with "That's *right*."

In these ways the children responded to what they heard without knowing the composer's story. They discovered rhythm and form. *The Nutcracker Suite* is also good program music, a type that will be discussed later.

Colored scarves are effective in phrase or theme recognition. Children may select one color for one theme and another color for another theme. They may merely swing the scarves or use them as they dance. They will think of many effective uses. Colored pompons serve the same purpose and add a pleasing swish which is effective with some music.

Children can create lovely dances by listening to the music. These created dances serve a number of purposes. They encourage purposeful listening, help develop muscular coordination, and are more satisfactory to the children than imposed directions. Often the results are practically the same as the traditional dances, yet the process is much more meaningful. If the children are listening to the music, they cannot forget what they are doing. At all times the children should be conscious of the relationship of the dance to the music. The rhythmic activity should be appropriate to the music.

Children in an upper grade enjoyed discovering each time the guard changed in "Soldiers Changing the Guard" from Bizet's *Carmen*. A different group marched at each entrance of the theme.

One class made their own minuet to Mozart's "Minuet" from *Don Giovanni*. They listened to the music and decided it was a stately stepping tune. As they stepped to the rhythm, several observed that the music paused at intervals. Some pointed their toes during these pauses, and a few curtsied and bowed. After some discussion the class decided they would point their toes on the short pauses and curtsy and bow on the long pauses. Further suggestions from the class developed a minuet very much like the traditional dance, yet much more meaningful to the children. Contrast this procedure with the one wherein the teacher recites, "Step, step, step, step and point," and the children merely follow directions.

The meaningful procedure described above is very successful in teaching folk dances. The children *feel* the rhythm and the phrases first, then create their own dances which may or may not be modified to imitate the traditional dances.

¶ USE OF INSTRUMENTS — Children enjoy using instruments to interpret music. There are a number of compositions using the clock. The music should be played first, and the children allowed to "discover" the clock and to discuss the *kind* of clock before the instruments are used.

"The Viennese Musical Clock," 2nd movement of the *Háry János Suite* by Kodály, calls for a ticking sound such as that made by sticks. Children may wish to march or to use drums for the miniature mechanical soldier figures which march around the clock. Chime effects may also be achieved, but care must be taken to keep the effect musical. A few chopsticks or the eraser ends of pencils will give a delicate ticking effect without covering the sound of the music.

Sand blocks can be used effectively with *The Little Train of Caipura* by Villa Lobos, "Departure" from *Winter Holiday* by Prokofiev, and *Pacific 231* by Honegger.

Undoubtedly children will want to play tiny sleigh bells during "The Sleighride" from *Eight German Dances* by Mozart. "Troika" from *Lieutenant Kijé Suite* by Prokofiev may also call for bells.

A teacher taught her third graders to play the theme from *Finlandia* on their song flutes:

One day as the children were working quietly at their seats, without saying a word the teacher° played the record. The children stopped their work and listened attentively to "their" tune. Several took out their music and followed it. The expressions on their faces would have delighted Sibelius himself.

Other themes this teacher used from time to time included Beethoven's *Ninth Symphony*, Fourth Movement; 1st theme:

and "Largo" from Dvořák's *Symphony No. 5* in E minor; Second Movement, 1st theme (transposed from D♭):

A teacher of an intermediate grade told her class the story of Beethoven's friend Maelzel and his invention, the metronome. The class lightly tapped their desks with pencils as they listened to the first theme of Beethoven's *Eighth Symphony*, Second Movement:

¶ DRAMATIZATION — There are many good compositions which lend themselves to dramatization. Either the children can make their own stories, or the teacher can tell them the story the composer had in mind.

° Miss Belle Piendl, first grade teacher, Roosevelt School, Spokane, Washington.

A sixth grade studies "Carmen"

Of a Tailor and a Bear by Edward MacDowell was used in this way by one teacher. He told part of the story and let the children supply the rest. He told them that the composer had in mind a tailor who was sitting in his shop sewing. The tailor whistled a little tune as he worked. He looked up and saw an animal standing in the doorway. At first the poor tailor was frightened, but then he saw a leash, or strap, dangling from the animal's neck. He decided that the animal must be tame and might like to do tricks, so he picked up his musical instrument and started to play. Sure enough, the animal started to do tricks.

The teacher then asked the children to listen to the music in order to discover:

1. The kind of animal in the story and the kind of tricks.
2. What instrument the tailor played.
3. What happened at the end.
4. What would be a good title for the music.

After listening to the music, the children decided it was a *big* animal, because they heard him growl in a low tone. Someone guessed it was a bear. The tailor was playing a *violin.* Finally the bear's owner *took him away* and the *tailor went back to work.* "The Tailor and the Dancing Bear" was suggested as a title for the music, for the music sounded like a clumsy dance. The teacher then told the class the real title and filled in the story, calling attention to the tuning of the violin. A papier mâché mask of a bear head helped in a dramatization of the story. The characters included the tailor, the bear and the owner of the bear.

¶ SINGING AND LISTENING — Children enjoy re-discovering songs which they have already learned. Some orchestral music which uses song material includes:

American Salute, Morton Gould
    When Johnny Comes Marching Home (20:20)
Billy the Kid, Ballet, 4th theme, Aaron Copland
    Good-by, Old Paint (24:38)
A Children's Overture, Roger Quilter
    Girls and Boys Come Out to Play (20:152)
    St. Paul's Steeple (21:3)
    Dame Get Up and Bake Your Pies (19:134)
    I Saw Three Ships (1:224) (19:57)
    Sing a Song of Sixpence (18:45)
    Over the Hills and Far Away (19:139)
    The Frog and the Crow (20:106)
    The Frog He Would A-wooing Go (20:126)
    Oranges and Lemons (19:92)
    Baa Baa Black Sheep (1:250)
A Cowboy Rhapsody, Morton Gould
    Good-by, Old Paint (24:38)
    Home on the Range (24:10)
Fantasy on Greensleeves, Vaughan-Williams,
    Greensleeves (7:28)
Hansel and Gretel, Prelude Act I, Humperdinck
    Prayer (2:178)
    Song of the Gingerbread Children (2:184)
A Lincoln Portrait, Aaron Copland
    Camptown Races (21:209)
    Pesky Sarpint, or Springfield Mountain (9:151)

Pop Goes the Weasel, Cailliet
>Pop Goes the Weasel (9:56)

Symphony No. 8, 2nd Movement, Beethoven
>The Metronome (26:47)

Symphony No. 5 in E Minor, 1st Movement, 3rd theme, Dvořák
>Swing Low, Sweet Chariot (27:82)

Turkey in the Straw, Guion
>Old Zip Coon (20:128)

Singing should not be restricted to song melodies only. An instrumental composition with a beautiful song-like melody should be hummed by the students as they hear it played. The student who leaves a music classroom humming one of the melodies he has heard, has undoubtedly been reached.

¶ FOLLOWING THE THEME — Themes may be written on the chalkboard or on tagboard. Tagboard may be preserved for future use. The teacher may play the themes on the piano or other instrument before the record is played. The children follow the written music as it is played. This prepares them for recognition of the themes in the entire composition. The themes are old friends in a new setting when heard on the phonograph. Children enjoy pointing to the theme as it is being played. This is a form of note reading. Children correlate what they hear with what they see. If the music goes up, down, or repeats, the notation does the same. This activity may be started in the primary grades. Music with definite contrasting themes should be used for first attempts.

"Minuet" from *Quintet in E Major* by Boccherini is a good number for theme recognition. The stage may be set by explaining that the minuet was danced in George Washington's time. The children listen to the music to see how they think the ladies and gentlemen danced. They will discover that the music is not too fast and is rather dainty, in keeping with the style of dress and the courtly manners of those days. The music seems to move in little steps. "Minuet" means "little steps." The class may also discover that the music swings in 3's. Thus far only the rhythm has been observed. This may be enough for the first lesson. If so, the record may be played again with rhythmic response.

Some child may have noticed that there are two tunes in this music. If not, the teacher may lead them to that discovery, or he may explain that the old minuets had two tunes or "themes." The second was called a trio, because it was played by three instruments. The teacher then plays a few measures of each theme in the *Minuet* as the children listen. (These themes should be written on tagboard, before class.)

1st Theme

2nd Theme

As the record is played children follow the themes with a pointer. One child may do this, or two different children may participate, each following one of the themes.

A primary teacher used pictures of a lady and a gentleman in Colonial dress. The children selected one for each theme and placed it on the flannel board as the corresponding theme was played.°

Various techniques may be used in theme following. In one class a different child held the chart for each theme and stepped forward whenever his theme was being played.

As the children become more adept at following themes visually, more complicated music may be used.

¶ PROGRAM OR STORY MUSIC — Program music is music in which the composer suggests a story or scene. High tones may be used to suggest height or distance. Soft music may also suggest distance. The rhythm may tell the listener that the characters are marching, dancing, working or sleeping. Some composers are extremely clever in communicating their ideas to the listeners.

Skillfully taught, program music may contribute definitely toward the musical development of the child. The teacher who merely

° Cortez Elementary School, Los Angeles, California, Mrs. Beatrice Grosbayne, Teacher.

tells the story and plays the record is not giving the children a creative experience. The children may complete the story several times before the music ends, or the music may end before they have completed the story. Failure to come out even with the music only causes the child to feel that music is not for him; he does not understand it. The teacher must make careful plans. (See pages 119-121.)

Children should be told what to listen for in the *order in which the musical effects occur in the composition.* The teacher should direct the listening, but should be careful not to give away the story.

After the music has been played, the first question should call for the *key* to the situation. Any arguments can be settled by referring to the music. Each listening lesson should end with listening to the record in its entirety.

Music and story

Lesson Plan for Listening to Program Music
(For upper grades)

Materials

Le Rouet d'Omphale or *Omphale's Spinning Wheel* by Saint-Saëns (Columbia or MSB)
Themes on tagboard
Pointer

Expected Outcomes

It is hoped that the class will
1. Become acquainted with and enjoy another good musical composition.
2. Learn to follow the story of the music through listening for effects.
3. Grow in ability to get a visual concept from an aural impression. ▸
4. Develop a deeper appreciation for music in general.

The Facts about the Music

Kinscella (15:66) tells us that this is the first of a series of four tone poems by Saint-Saëns. It was first performed as a piano solo in 1871. The following year it was enthusiastically received by Paris at the Concert Populaire.

The composition begins with muted strings alternating with the flutes in quiet music which becomes livelier. The higher wind instruments embellish the main theme while the horn accents the meter.

A series of episodical harmonies, Omphale's maidens singing, introduces a lovely melody in the wind section with occasional strings. As this song is repeated the harp adds showers of notes in harmony, the drum is lightly tapped, and the trumpet sounds a single tone.

Hercules' air is now heard in the lower instruments of the strings, woodwinds, and brasses, accompanied by the soft clashing of cymbals. As the song becomes more intense, trumpets blare and the drums increase.

Hercules has been unable to break loose, and again we hear the whirr of the spinning wheel and the laughter of the maidens in the flutes and harp.

As the day ends, the maidens, one by one, stop their work.

Tovey (25:21) objects to "oiliness and stickiness" even if associated with admirable techniques; however, he speaks of *Le Rouet d'Omphale* as being, "damned clever."

O'Connell (23) claims that Hercules masqueraded as a woman to escape "unpleasant circumstances." Omphale put him to work spinning. The strings portray the whirring wheel and the mournful theme depicts Hercules in distress.

The Program Notes of the Los Angeles Symphony (16) tell us that Hercules became very ill when he learned that he had slain his friend, Iphitus, in a fit of madness. The Delphic Oracle promised to restore his health if he atoned by serving three years for wages. Consequently Hercules worked for Omphale, spinning wool with her maidens and wearing effeminate clothing.

The program notes of the Chicago Symphony (7) give us the words of Saint-Saëns, himself:

"The subject of this orchestral poem is feminine seductiveness, the triumphant struggle of weakness with strength. The Spinning Wheel is but a pretext, chosen merely from the point of view of rhythm and of the general physiognomy of the composition.

"Persons who are desirous of going more into detail will find on p. 19 (letter J) Hercules groaning under the bonds he cannot break, and on p. 32 (letter L) Omphale laughing at the hero's futile efforts."

One commentator (Maczewski) . . . in the light of the foregoing detects three themes of illustrative significance, as follows:

1. The power of feminine allurement triumphant in the struggle of weakness against strength; in fact, Omphale's fascination of Hercules.
2. Hercules in bondage.
3. Omphale deriding the efforts of the hero.

Procedure

Have the themes visible to the class.

"Our music today tells us a story. We shall see how good you are as detectives. I shall give you a few clues. Let's listen to the pitch of the introduction and show it with our hands." Play the following on the bells, the piano, or other instrument.

Students discover that the music goes up and down regularly.

"What kind of persons do you think the music represents here?"

Children say the persons are young and gay. How can they tell? The music is quick, high and light.

"Now listen to this music and see what kind of person this represents."

Class thinks it is a big man; the music is low in pitch. He is strong; the music is stronger, louder. He is sad; the music is heavy and slow. (Theme I is major and Theme II is minor, but students must not get the idea that *all* minor music is sad.)

"Now that you have some of the clues, I am going to tell you part of the story, and we shall see if you can finish it."

"Once upon a time, long ago, there was a big strong man named Hercules. He was so big and strong that he did not realize his own strength, and one day as he was quarreling with a friend he accidentally killed him. In punishment Hercules was sent to become a slave to a queen named Omphale. Omphale was a cruel woman. She made Hercules dress as one of her serving maids and do the same kind of work the maids did. In this music you will hear Hercules trying to do this work.

"That first music that you heard which went up and down in regular rhythm will tell you the kind of work it was. It was something that we do not have to do today, but our great-great grandmothers had to do it when they came over to this country in Colonial days.

"Next the music will tell you how the queen and her maids acted when Hercules was working.

"You said that Hercules seemed unhappy. You are right. He was in chains. Let us see if you can tell what he tried to do about his predicament.

"Finally, let us see if Hercules was successful."

Play the record.

"What kind of work did Hercules have to do?"
    "How did the music start?" . . . Slowly.
    "Then what happened?" . . . It gradually became faster.
        (If the class does not get this point, play the music again and have
        them use their arms up and down with the music in regular rhythm.
        They should get the feeling of a turning wheel. Some will hear the
        whirr.)
"Did the music tell you how the maids and Omphale reacted to Hercules' spin-
    ning?" They laughed at him.
"What did the music do?" There were quick little high notes. There was also
    a melody as though they sang.
"What did Hercules try to do about his predicament?" He tried to break away.
    You could feel the music becoming louder and stronger as though he were
    bulging his muscles and straining at his chains. More instruments were
    added to help the music become louder.
"Did the music continue loud until the end?" No, it faded out.
"Did it fade out on Hercules' tune, or did it change?" It returned to the first
    melody.
"What do you think happened?" He had to give up and return to his spinning,
    with the maids laughing again.
"If he had broken away, how do you think the music might have shown it?"
    The queen might have called out the soldiers.

Play the record again and let the students point to the themes. Students may
    hum the melody the maids sing and the Hercules melody.

Follow-up questions for a later listening:
    "Did you hear anything else while Hercules was trying to break away?"
    A violin played his melody up high.
    "What do you think that might have represented?" Perhaps one of the
    maids sympathized with him.

"What happened at the very end?" The music gradually faded out, as though the maids were quitting, one by one, and calling out good-bys or giggling as they left.

(Always replay the record when there is a doubt.)

EVALUATION

1. Did the class enjoy the music?
2. Were the children able to follow the story through the music?
3. Were they able to follow the themes?
4. Does the class want to hear the music again at another time?

Form in Listening

¶ CANON — Form has already been discussed as theme recognition, but it can be developed further. One form which children in the elementary school can understand and enjoy is the *canon*. Anyone who has sung rounds can understand a canon. The first movement of *Pop Goes the Weasel,* arranged by Lucien Cailliet, closes as a canon, that is, each voice takes up the melody in turn while the other voices continue. Children can recognize each entrance of the main melody. "Nocturne" from the *String Quartet No. 2 in D Major* by Borodin also utilizes the canon.

¶ FUGUE — A *fugue* (derived from the Latin *fuga,* meaning *flight*) is similar to a *round.* An instrumental fugue is a sort of canon in which instruments become the "voices." The theme or musical subject may be introduced by one instrument (or group of instruments) then taken up by another, and so on. After all the voices have entered in succession, there follows a passage wherein this subject is developed, or worked out. After this, the subject returns in the same or a similar treatment. This results in a three-part form, A B A′. Toward the end of this re-entry occurs the *stretto,* which is merely an overlapping of the themes much in the nature of a round such as *Three Blind Mice.* Instead of each voice ending separately as is usually the case in the round, the voices in the fugue all end together. Examples of the fugue include:

The Gossips by Dubensky
The Cat's Fugue by Scarlatti
Fugato on a Well-known Theme by McBride

The most important point for children to understand in the fugue is the entrance of the subject. Benjamin Britten's *The Young Person's Guide to the Orchestra*, on a theme by Purcell, uses the fugue to introduce the different sections of the orchestra. The film is even better, because it shows each section of the orchestra as it takes up the subject. *Little Fugue in G Minor* also shows the sections of the orchestra in this way.

¶ THEME AND VARIATIONS — In this form the Theme is stated first and then varied in either melody, rhythm, or harmony. *Pop Goes the Weasel*, arranged for orchestra by Lucien Cailliet, is a good example of this form. The first movement was discussed as a canon (p. 137). Variation I is a lively dance, a *gigue*. Variation II is a *minuet*, Variation III, a minor adagio labeled "In Jerusalem." Variation IV is called "Music Box," Variation V "In Jazz," and the Coda or "tail" is a return to fugue or canon.

The important point in the study of this form is the development of the ability to discover the *manner* in which the theme has been changed. Children can be detectives trying to discover the theme disguised in the variation. Perhaps the accent or the tempo has been changed. Perhaps the melody has been inverted (turned upside down), or written in retrograde (backwards). Changes in harmony may be achieved by use of the canon or fugue. Changing from major to minor and vice versa is a common means of variation. Tone color may be varied by giving the melody to various instruments and building harmonies or accompaniments with other instruments. Counter melodies may be used. It is quite common for a concert artist to play a theme in the styles of Bach, Chopin, Schubert, Debussy or Gershwin. Each style would be a variation.

Choosing Background Music

From time to time background music is needed for dramatizations, puppet shows, and creative rhythms. Children should be encouraged to make the selections. This activity stimulates listening to a great many recordings and also helps to develop powers of discrimination. Often the children will discover other music which piques their curiosity. They want to play it for the class and learn more about it.

Older children find background music for current films interesting. The magazine, *Film Notes* (8), is helpful.

*The fun of listening
at home with Mom*

Concerts

In addition to phonograph records there are other sources of listening for children. Artists within the community will often play or sing for the school which their children, or the children of their friends attend. Little informal chats about the instruments the artists use fascinate children.

Sometimes upper grade children or high school students can give profitable and enjoyable informal recitals for the younger children. Listening to each other is also a fine activity. Many youngsters take class or private music lessons and should be encouraged to play for their schoolmates. Occasionally a very talented child is shy in a group. Playing for his classmates may be the key by which he enters into the group. A little boost to his ego may help him immeasurably.

Some radio programs contribute to the listening activities. Each area has its own programs such as Standard School Broadcast in the West, Symphonies for Youth in Los Angeles. Sometimes The Telephone Hour correlates a special program with the music magazines for children, *Keyboard Jr,* and *Young Keyboard Jr.* It is to be hoped that television will become a source of good listening.

Children should be encouraged to report on concerts they have attended or heard. Bulletin board space may be reserved for newspaper and magazine clippings or pictures about music. Occasionally a child hears on radio or television a composition he has studied in class. He should have an opportunity to tell about it.

Time should be set aside for children to listen to records of their choice. These may be selected by different small groups within the class, or the class as a whole may select their favorites among the records heard during the month or semester.

Reading Material for Children

Today there are a great many excellent books about music and composers written especially for children. Schools are always looking for good biographies for children to read. The biographies written by Opal Wheeler, Sybil Deucher, Clair Lee Purdy and many others are fascinating reading material for children and should be made available to them. (See pp. 147, 148.)

Young Keyboard Jr (28) is a little music magazine for elementary school children. It is published monthly from October to May and contains both old and current information about music. *Keyboard Jr* is the same type of magazine, but geared to the interests of junior and senior high school students.

¶ CONCLUSION — Creativity in lesson planning comes from intelligent experimentation and evaluation. The suggestions given here are intended merely as a springboard from which it is hoped that future teachers may be encouraged to plunge and to explore the vast possibilities for themselves and their students. The wise teacher will *first* choose the *music, then* the *approach.*

Questions for Class Discussion

1. Some educators believe that children appreciate only the music they themselves sing or play. What do you think?
2. Other educators believe that listening is the core of every musical experience. What do you believe?
3. What phases of discriminative listening can be successfully introduced in:
   A. Early childhood

B. The intermediate grades
C. The upper grades
4. How have radio and television affected listening habits?
5. How can the talents of the home room, other classes, parents, and neighbors contribute to the school listening experiences?
6. How can current movies be utilized in the listening experiences?

Written Assignments

1. List all radio programs which you think can contribute to the listening program.
2. List all television programs which you think are musically suitable for children.
3. Familiarize yourself with the RCA Basic Educational Record Library. Choose one lesson which you think would appeal especially to children of a specific grade of your choice. Give a brief review of the lesson and tell why you chose it.
4. Familiarize yourself with the Young People's Records, Musical Sound Books, and the Children's Guild Records. Choose one you especially like, and tell why you chose it.
5. Make two complete lesson plans of your own. (See pp. 118-121.) Use a different type of approach for each.

Bibliography

1. Armitage, Theresa et al, *Our First Music*. Boston: C. C. Birchard & Co., 1941.
2. Armitage, Theresa et al, *We Sing*. Boston: C. C. Birchard & Co., 1940, 1953.
3. Baldwin, Lillian, Music for Young Listeners, *The Blue Book*. New York: Silver Burdett Co., 1951.
4. Baldwin, Lillian, Music for Young Listeners, *The Crimson Book*. New York: Silver Burdett Co., 1951.
5. Baldwin, Lillian, Music for Young Listeners, *The Green Book*. New York: Silver Burdett Co., 1951.
6. Barlow, Harold, and Morgenstern, Sam, *A Dictionary of Musical Themes*. New York: Crown Publishing Co., 1948.
7. *Chicago Symphony Orchestra Programs*, XII. Orchestral Ass'n., 650 Orchestra Hall, 220 South Michigan Ave., Chicago, Ill.
8. *Film Notes*, 31 Union Square West, New York, New York; published 3 times yearly.
9. Fullerton, Margaret and Wolfe, Irving, *Together We Sing*. Chicago: Follett Publishing Co., 1950.
10. Hartshorn, William and Leavitt, Helen, *The Mentor,* Making Friends with Music. Boston: Ginn & Co., 1940.
11. Hartshorn, William and Leavitt, Helen, *The Pilot,* Making Friends with Music. Boston: Ginn & Co., 1940.
12. House, Margueritte, *O Say Can You Hear?* Bks. 1, 2, 3, 4. New York: Mills Music Co., 1947, 1949, 1952.
13. Hughes, Langston, *The First Book of Jazz*. New York: Franklin Watts, Inc., 1955.
14. Ives, Burl, *The Burl Ives Song Book*. New York: Ballantine Books, 1953.
15. Kinscella, Hazel Gertrude, *Music and Romance*. Camden, N. J.: RCA Victor Publishing Co., 1941.

16. *Los Angeles Symphony Programs,* 1931-32, 8th Sunday. Los Angeles: Huber Publications.
17. McConathy, Osbourne et al, *New Music Horizons,* Bk. I. New York: Silver Burdett Co., 1944.
18. McConathy, Osbourne et al, *New Music Horizons,* Bk. III. New York: Silver Burdett Co., 1944.
19. McConathy, Osbourne et al, *New Music Horizons,* Bk. IV. New York: Silver Burdett Co., 1945.
20. McConathy, Osbourne et al, *New Music Horizons,* Bk. V. New York: Silver Burdett Co., 1946.
21. McConathy, Osbourne et al, *New Music Horizons,* Bk. VI. New York: Silver Burdett Co., 1946.
22. Mursell, James et al, *Music Around the World,* New York: Silver Burdett Co., 1956.
23. O'Connell, Charles, *The Victor Book of Overtures, Tone Poems and Other Orchestral Works.* New York: Simon & Schuster, Inc., 1941.
24. Pitts, Lilla Belle et al, *Singing Every Day.* Boston: Ginn & Co., 1950.
25. Tovey, Sir Donald Francis, *Essays in Musical Analysis.* Vol. 1. London: Oxford University Press, 1939.
26. Wilson, Harry, *Rounds and Canons.* Chicago: Hall & McCreary Co., 1943.
27. Wilson, Harry, *Sing Along.* New York: J. J. Robbins and Sons, Inc., 1948.
28. *Young Keyboard Jr.,* 1346 Chapel St., New Haven 11, Conn.

RECORDINGS AND FILMS

Bach, J. S., *Little Fugue in G Minor,* Stokowski conducting. (Victor record.) Film — Teaching Film Custodians, Inc., 25 West 43rd St., New York 18, N. Y.

Beethoven, Ludwig van
Symphony No. 8, Toscanini conducting. (Victor)
Symphony No. 9, Toscanini conducting. (Victor)

Boccherini, Luigi
"Minuet" from *Quintet in E Major* (Musical Sound Books for Young Listeners) (RCA Elementary School Library)

Borodin, Alexander
Polovtzian Dances. (Capitol)
String Quartet No. 2 in D Major. (Period)

Cailliet, Lucien
Pop Goes the Weasel. Boston Pops Orchestra (Victor)

Copland, Aaron
A Lincoln Portrait (Columbia)
Billy the Kid (Victor)

Dubensky, Arcady
The Gossips (Musical Sound Books)

Dvořák, Anton
Symphony No. 5 in E minor (Victor)

Gould, Morton
American Salute (Columbia)
Cowboy Rhapsody (Columbia)

Guion, David
Turkey in the Straw (Musical Sound Books) (RCA Elementary School Library)

Haydn, Joseph
Symphony in D, "The Clock" (Westminster)

Honegger, Arthur
Pacific 231; Film — Franco American AVC 1950.

Humperdinck, Engelbert
Prelude Act I, Hansel and Gretel
Jazz Band, Young Peoples' Record

Kodály, Zoltan
Háry János Suite, Pt. II, *The Viennese Musical Clock* (Columbia) (Victor)

MacDowell, Edward
Of a Tailor and a Bear (Musical Sound Books) (RCA Elementary School Library)

McBride, Robert
Fugato on a Well-Known Theme (Victor)

Mozart, Wolfgang Amadeus
The "Sleigh Ride" from *Eight German Dances.* (Musical Sound Books)
"Minuet" from *Don Giovanni* (Musical Sound Books) (RCA Elementary School Library)

Prokofiev, Serge
"Departure" from *Winter Holiday Suite*
"Troika" from *Lieutenant Kijé Suite* (Westminster)

Purcell-Britten
Young Person's Guide to the Orchestra, The (Columbia)

The Instruments of the Orchestra
(Film), British Information Service,
1947. 20 min.
Quilter, Roger
   A Children's Overture (Musical Sound
   Books)
Saint-Saëns, Camille
   Le Rouet d'Omphale, Op. 31 (Colum-
   bia) (Musical Sound Books)
Scarlatti, Domenico
   The Cat's Fugue (Musical Sound
   Books)
Schubert, Franz
   Quintet in A Major, 4th Movement
   (Columbia)
Sibelius, Jean
   Finlandia (Columbia) (Victor)
The Story of Jazz, narrated by Langston
Hughes (Folkways)
Tchaikovsky, Peter
   "March" from the *Nutcracker Suite*
   (RCA Elementary School Library)
   (Musical Sound Books)
Vaughan Williams, Ralph
   Fantasia on "Greensleeves" (London)
   (Musical Sound Books)
Villa-Lobos, Heitor
   The Little Train of Caipura (Capitol)

SUGGESTED RECORDINGS FOR
LISTENING LESSONS

Air from Suite #3 in D (Air for G
   String), Bach
Amaryllis, Ghys
Andante Cantabile, Tchaikovsky
Andante from *The Surprise Symphony,*
   Haydn
"Anitra's Dance" from *Peer Gynt Suite
   No. 1,* Grieg
"Arab Dance" from the *Nutcracker
   Suite,* Tchaikovsky
Arkansas Traveler, The, Guion
Ave Maria, Bach-Gounod
Ave Maria, Schubert

Baby's Family, The, Villa-Lobos
Bachianas Brasilieras, No. 1, Villa-Lobos
Ballet Music from *Faust,* Gounod
"Billy the Kid" Suite, Copland
Blue Danube Waltz, J. Strauss
Bolero, Ravel

Carnival of the Animals, Saint-Saëns
Cat's Fugue, The, Scarlatti

Children's Corner Suite, The, Debussy
   Golliwog's Cakewalk
   Jumbo's Lullaby
   Little Shepherd, The
Children's Games, Bizet
Children's Overture, Quilter
Christmas Hymns and Carols (Robert
   Shaw Chorale)
Cinderella, Prokofiev
Cinderella Fantasy, Coates
Claire de Lune, Debussy
Concerto for Piano, Op. 16, Grieg
Country Gardens, arranged by Percy
   Grainger
Cowboy Rhapsody, Gould

"Dance of the Buffoons" from *The Snow
   Maiden,* Rimsky-Korsakov
"Dance of the Comedians" from *The
   Bartered Bride,* Smetana
"Dance of the Flutes" from the *Nut-
   cracker Suite,* Tchaikovsky
"Dance of the Hours" from *La Gioconda,*
   Ponchielli
"Dance of the Sugar Plum Fairy" from
   the *Nutcracker Suite,* Tchaikovsky
Dancing Doll, Poldini
Danse Macabre, Saint-Saëns
Death Valley Suite, Ferde Grofé
"Departure" from *Winter Holiday,*
   Prokofiev

Eight German Dances, Mozart
"Entr'acte and Valse" from *Coppelia,*
   Délibes
España, Rhapsody for Orchestra, Chab-
   rier
"Evening Prayer" from *Hansel and
   Gretel,* Humperdinck

Fantasia on "Greensleeves," Vaughan
   Williams
"Festival March" from *Tannhäuser,* Wag-
   ner
Finlandia, Sibelius
Fingal's Cave Overture, Mendelssohn
Flight of the Bumble Bee, Rimsky-Kor-
   sakov
"Folk Song" from *Hansel and Gretel,*
   Humperdinck
From Childhood, Harl McDonald
From the Canebrake, Gardner
Fugato on a Well-known Theme, Mc-
   Bride
Funeral March of a Marionette, Gounod

Gossips, The, Dubensky
Grand Canyon Suite, Grofé

"Hallelujah Chorus" from the *Messiah*, Handel
Hansel and Gretel Prelude, Humperdinck
Hansel and Gretel Selections, Humperdinck
Háry János Suite, Kodály
"He Shall Feed His Flock" from the *Messiah*, Handel
Hungarian Dances Nos. 5 and 6, Brahms
"Hut of Baba Yaga" from *Pictures at an Exhibition*, Mussorgsky

"If With All Your Hearts" from *Elijah*, Mendelssohn
"In the Hall of the Mountain King" from *Peer Gynt Suite No. 1*, Grieg
In the Steppes of Central Asia, Borodin
"In the Village" from *Caucasian Sketches*, Ippolitov-Ivanov
Invitation to the Dance, von Weber

Jeux d'eau, Debussy
Juba Dance, Dett

La Cathédrale Engloutie (The Sunken Cathedral), Debussy
La Mer, Debussy
"Largo" from *Xerxes*, Handel
Le Rouet d'Omphale (Omphale's Spinning Wheel), Saint-Saëns
Liebesträume, Liszt
Little Fugue in G Minor, Bach
Little Train of Caipura, The, Villa-Lobos
London Suite, Coates
Londonderry Air, arranged by Percy Grainger
Love of Three Oranges, The, Prokofiev
    March
    Scherzo
Lullaby, Brahms

"March" from the *Nutcracker Suite*, Tchaikovsky
March of the Dwarfs, Grieg
March of the Little Lead Soldiers, Pierné
March Slav, Tchaikovsky
March of the Toys, Victor Herbert
Marche Militaire, Schubert
"Minuet" from *Don Giovanni*, Mozart
"Minuet" from *Quintet in E Major*, Boccherini
Molly on the Shore, arranged by Percy

Grainger
Mother Goose Suite (Ma Mère L'Oye), Ravel
Musical Snuff-Box, A, Liadoff

Night on Bald Mountain, Mussorgsky
"Nocturne" from *String Quartet No. 2 in D Major*, Borodin
Norwegian Bridal Procession, Grieg
Norwegian Dance No. 2, Grieg
Nutcracker Suite, Tchaikovsky
    Overture Miniature
    March
    Dance of the Sugar Plum Fairy
    Trepak
    Arab Dance
    Chinese Dance
    Dance of the Flutes
    Waltz of the Flowers

Of a Tailor and a Bear, MacDowell
Of Br'er Rabbit, MacDowell

Peer Gynt Suite, No. 1, Grieg
    Morning Mood
    The Death of Ase
    Anitra's Dance
    In the Hall of the Mountain King
Peter and the Wolf, Prokofiev
Pictures at an Exhibition, Mussorgsky
Pleasure Dome of Kubla Khan, The, Griffes
"Polka" from *The Golden Age*, Shostakovich
Polka and Fugue from *Schwanda, the Bagpiper*, Weinberger
"Polovtzian Dances" from *Prince Igor*, Borodin
Pomp and Circumstance #1 and #4, Elgar
Pop Goes the Weasel, Cailliet
Prelude from Act I, *Lohengrin*, Wagner
Prelude from Act III, *Lohengrin*, Wagner
"Procession of the Sardar" from *Caucasian Sketches*, Ippolitov-Ivanov

Quintet in A Major, 4th Movement (The Trout), Schubert

Rákóczy March from *Damnation of Faust*, Berlioz
Rhapsody in Blue, Gershwin
Rock-A-Bye Baby

Scenes from Childhood, Schumann

Scheherazade, Rimsky-Korsakoff

Skaters' Waltz, The, Waldteufel

Song of the Volga Boatman

Songs of the African Veld, sung by Marais and Miranda

Sorcerer's Apprentice, The, Dukas

Stars and Stripes Forever, The, Sousa

Sunken Cathedral, The, Debussy

Swan Lake, Tchaikovsky

Symphony No. 5, 1st Movement (Fate), Beethoven

Symphony No. 8, 2nd Movement (Maelzel's Metronome), Beethoven

Symphony No. 9, 4th Movement (Choral), Beethoven

Symphony in E Minor (New World), Dvorák

Symphony 94 in G Major, 2nd Movement (Surprise), Haydn

Symphony in B Minor, No. 8 (Unfinished), Schubert

Syncopated Clock, The, Leroy Anderson

Tales of the Vienna Woods, J. Strauss

Till Eulenspiegel's Merry Pranks, R. Strauss

"Toreador Song" from Carmen, Bizet

Toy Symphony, Haydn

Tritsch-Tratsch Polka, J. Strauss

Triumphal March from Aida, Verdi

Turkey in the Straw, Guion

"Troika" from Lieutenant Kijé Suite, Prokofiev

Western Symphony, Kay

White Peacock, The, Griffes

William Tell Overture, Rossini

Witches' Dance, MacDowell

"Witches' Sabbath" from Fantastic Symphony, Berlioz

RECORDS ABOUT COMPOSERS AND MUSIC

Aaron Copland, The Music of (with music about America) (Young People's Records)

Chopin (Story and Music) narrated by Milton Cross (Columbia)

Haydn (Story and Music), narrated by Milton Cross (Columbia)

Mozart (Story and Music), narrated by Milton Cross (Columbia)

Composer Series (Vox recordings)
1. Bach, His Story and His Music
2. Mozart

3. Beethoven
4. Schubert
5. Mendelssohn
6. Chopin
7. Brahms
8. Schumann
9. Tchaikovsky
10. Strauss
11. Grieg
12. Stephen Foster
13. Liszt
14. Berlioz
15. Paganini

The Composer, His Life, His Times, His Music Series (upper grades), narrated by David Randolph (Period)
Haydn, Mozart, Beethoven, Chopin, Schubert, Tchaikovsky, Brahms, Schumann, Bach

Piano Adventures, narrated by Mary Van Doren (Mercury)
Schumann, Grieg, Bach, Beethoven, Mendelssohn, MacDowell, Haydn, Debussy, Mozart

Musical Sound Books, based on Lillian Baldwin's Books (MSB).
The Blue Book
The Crimson Book
The Green Book
The Brown Book (Music to Remember)

RCA Library for Elementary Schools
Listening Activities   Albums 1-6
Rhythmic Activities   Albums 1-6
Singing Activities   4 Albums

Round and Round (explains round, canon and fugue) (Young People's Records)

Jazz Band (Young People's Records)

The Story of Jazz for Children, narrated by Langston Hughes (Folkways)

RECORDS ABOUT INSTRUMENTS

The Child's Introduction to the Orchestra, Golden Record Chest (Simon & Schuster)

Concerto for Toys and Orchestra, YPR

First Chair (8 instrumental solos), Columbia

Hunter's Horn, The (French horn), YPR

Instruments of the Orchestra, Columbia

King's Trumpet, The, YPR

Licorice Stick (clarinet), YPR

Little Brass Band (primary), YPR

Little Indian Drum (primary), YPR
Rhythm Instruments, Ruth White, Rhythm Productions
Rondo for Bassoon and Orchestra, YPR
Rusty in Orchestraville, Capitol
Said the Piano to the Harpsichord, YPR
Sparky's Magic Piano, Capitol
Strike up the Band (primary), YPR
Tubby the Tuba, Capitol
Wonderful Violin, The, YPR
Young Person's Guide to the Orchestra, The, Columbia

ETHNIC MUSIC

(Music of various parts of the world, recorded on the spot)

Folkways Records of ethnic music of Cuba, Haiti, India, Jamaica, Japan, Korea, France, Australia, Spain, Negro Folk Music, Sioux and Navajo Indians, Eskimos, and many others.
Jungle Drums, Decca
World Library of Folk and Primitive Music collected and edited by Alan Lomax, Columbia

FILMS

Children's Concert, primary-upper grades, Encyclopaedia Britannica Films, Inc., 1950, 3 reels, 10-12 min.
Building Children's Personalities with Creative Dancing, Los Angeles: University of California, Dept. of Cinema.
First Chair, intermediate-upper grades, C. G. Conn, Ltd., 1947. On loan, apply. 37 min.

Great Waltz, The, upper grades, Teaching Films Custodians, 1949. On rental, apply. 20 min.
Hymn of the Nations (with Toscanini), upper grades, Brandon, 1945. 35 min.
Inside Opera (with Grace Moore), upper grades, Teaching Films Custodians, 1949. 29 min.
Instruments of the Orchestra, intermediate — upper grades, British Information Service, 1949. 20 min.
Little Fugue in G Minor by Bach, intermediate-upper grades, Teaching Films Custodians, 1951. On rental, apply. 4 min.
Magic Fire Spell, The, by Wagner, Clune Studios. Color. 10 min.
Merry Christmas, with Vienna Choir Boys, all levels, Sterling, 1949. 12 min.
Pacific 231, by Honegger, Franco-American AVC, 1950. Subscription basis, apply. 10 min.
Rhythm Instruments and Movement, Mahnke — Encyclopaedia Britannica Films, 1950. 10 min.
Science in the Orchestra, intermediate-upper grades, British Information Service, 1951. 3 reels, 15 min.
Silent Night, the Story of the Christmas Carol, Coronet. Black and white, 18 min.
Singing Pipes (pipe organ), upper grades, National Film Board of Canada. 20 min.
Story of a Violin (making a violin), intermediate-upper grades, National Film Board of Canada, 1948. 21 min.

General References

Adams, Fay, Educating America's Children. New York: Ronald Press, 1946, pp. 426-431.
Armitage, Theresa et al, Teachers' Manuals I-VI, Singing School Series. Boston: C. C. Birchard & Co., 1948.
Beattie, John W. et al, Teachers' Guides I-VI, American Singer Series. New York: American Book Co., 1947.
Buchanan, Fannie, How Man Made Music. Chicago: Follett Publishing Co., 1954.

Dykema, Peter W. and Cundiff, Hannah M., School Music Handbook. Boston: C. C. Birchard & Co., 1955.
Grant, Parks, Music for Elementary Teachers. New York: Appleton-Century-Crofts, Inc., 1951, Ch. XXVI.
*Hallstrom, John, Relax and Listen. New York: Rinehart & Co., 1947.
Howard, John T., Our American Music. New York: Thomas Y. Crowell Co., 1946.
Krone, Beatrice Perham, Music in the

*out of print

New School. Chicago: Neil A. Kjos Music Co., revised 1947, Ch. VIII.

Landeck, Beatrice, Children and Music. New York: William Sloane Associates, 1952, pp. 87-104.

Mathews, Paul W., You Can Teach Music. New York: E. P. Dutton & Co., 1953, Ch. VI.

McConathy, Osbourne et al, Teachers' Manuals, Primary and Intermediate. New Music Horizons Series. New York: Silver Burdett Co., 1948.

McKinney, Howard D., Music and Man. New York: American Book Co., 1948.

Mursell, James L., Education for Musical Growth. Boston: Ginn & Co., 1948, pp. 138-139, 168, 271-272, 281-283, 141-142.

Mursell, James L., Music and the Classroom Teacher. New York: Silver Burdett Co., 1951, Ch. V.

Myers, Louise Kifer, Teaching Children Music in the Elementary School. New York: Prentice-Hall, Inc., 1956, Ch. II, VI.

Pitts, Lilla Belle et al, Guide and Teaching Suggestions, Grades, Kindergarten — 3, 4-6, Our Singing World Series. Boston: Ginn & Co., 1950.

Sachs, Curt, Our Musical Heritage. Prentice-Hall, Inc., 1948, 1955.

Skolsky, Syd, Evenings with Music. New York: E. P. Dutton & Co., Inc. 1945.

Skolsky, Syd, Make Way for Music. New York: E. P. Dutton & Co., Inc., 1946

Stringham, Edwin J., Listening to Music Creatively. New York: Prentice-Hall, Inc., 1946.

Victor Book of the Opera. New York: Simon & Schuster, Inc., 1949.

Books for Children

Bakeless, Katherine, Story Lives of Great Composers. New York: Frederick A. Stokes Co., 1940, 1953.

Balet, Jan, What Makes an Orchestra. New York: Oxford University Press, 1951.

Buchanan, Fannie R., How Man Made Music. Chicago: Follett Publishing Co., 1954.

Burch, Gladys, Famous Pianists for Young People. New York: Dodd, Mead & Co., 1945.

Burch, Gladys, Famous Violinists for Young People. New York: Dodd, Mead & Co., 1946.

Burch, Gladys, Modern Composers for Young People. New York: Dodd, Mead & Co., 1941.

Burch, Gladys, Richard Wagner Who Followed a Star. New York: Henry Holt & Co., Inc., 1941.

Burch, Gladys, and Wolcott, John, Famous Composers for Young People. New York: Dodd, Mead & Co., 1945.

*Coit, Lottie E., and Bampton, Ruth, The Child Bach. Bryn Mawr, Pa.: Theodore Presser Co., 1943.

*Coit, Lottie E. and Bampton, Ruth, The Child Handel. Bryn Mawr, Pa.: Theodore Presser Co., 1945.

*Coit, Lottie E. and Bampton, Ruth, The Child Haydn. Bryn Mawr, Pa.: Theodore Presser Co., 1944.

*Coit, Lottie E. and Bampton, Ruth, The Child Mozart. Bryn Mawr, Pa.: Theodore Presser Co., 1942.

Ewen, David, Haydn, A Good Life. New York: Henry Holt & Co., 1946.

Ewen, David, The Story of George Gershwin. New York: Henry Holt & Co., 1943.

Ewen, David, The Story of Irving Berlin. New York: Henry Holt & Co., 1950.

Ewen, David, Tales from the Vienna Woods. New York: Henry Holt & Co., 1944.

Huntington, Harriet E., Tune Up. Garden City, N. Y.: Doubleday & Co., 1942.

Kinscella, Hazel, Folk Tales of Many Lands. Lincoln, Nebr.: University Publishing Co., 1951.

Kinscella, Hazel, History Sings. (Backgrounds of American Music). Lincoln, Nebr.: University Publishing Co., 1948.

Kinscella, Hazel, Tales of Olden Days. Lincoln, Nebr.: University Publishing Co., 1950.

Lacey, Marion, Picture Book of Musical Instruments. New York: Lothrop, Lee & Shepard Co., 1942.

Posell, Elsa Z., This Is an Orchestra. Boston: Houghton Mifflin Co., 1950.

Prokofiev, Serge, Peter and the Wolf. New York: Alfred A. Knopf, Inc., 1940.

Purdy, Clair Lee, He Heard America

---

*out of print

Sing, Life of Stephen Foster. New York: Julian Messner, Inc., 1940.

Purdy, Clair Lee, *Song of the North*, Edvard Grieg. New York: Julian Messner, Inc., 1941.

Purdy, Clair Lee, *Stormy Victory*, Tchaikovsky. New York: Julian Messner, Inc., 1945.

Purdy, Clair Lee, *Victor Herbert*. New York: Julian Messner, Inc., 1944.

Schwimmer, Francesca, *Great Musicians as Children*. Garden City, N. Y.: Doubleday & Co., 1927, 1946.

Skolsky, Syd, *The Music Box Book*. New York: E. P. Dutton & Co., 1946.

Wheeler, Opal, *Frederic Chopin, Son of Poland*. New York: E. P. Dutton & Co., 1948.

Wheeler, Opal, *Paganini, Master of Strings*. New York: E. P. Dutton & Co., 1950.

Wheeler, Opal, *Robert Schumann and his Mascot, Ziff*. New York: E. P. Dutton & Co., 1947.

Wheeler, Opal, *Stephen Foster and His Little Dog Tray*. New York: E. P. Dutton & Co., 1941.

Wheeler, Opal and Deucher, Sybil, *Edward MacDowell and His Cabin in the Pines*. New York: E. P. Dutton & Co., 1940.

Wheeler, Opal and Deucher, Sybil, *Franz Schubert and His Merry Little Friends*. New York: E. P. Dutton & Co., 1939.

Wheeler, Opal and Deucher, Sybil, *Handel at the Court of Kings*. New York: E. P. Dutton & Co., 1943.

Wheeler, Opal and Deucher, Sybil, *Joseph Haydn, the Merry Little Peasant*. New York: E. P. Dutton & Co., 1936.

Wheeler, Opal and Deucher, Sybil, *Ludwig Beethoven and the Chiming Tower Bells*. New York: E. P. Dutton & Co., 1942.

Wheeler, Opal and Deucher, Sybil, *Mozart, the Wonder Boy*. New York: E. P. Dutton & Co., 1934, 1941.

Wheeler, Opal and Deucher, Sybil, *Sebastian Bach, the Boy from Thuringia*. New York: E. P. Dutton & Co., 1937.

Creative rhythms

CHAPTER VI

Let's Make Our Own Music

Creative activities include more than making songs. All music is either creative or re-creative.

Re-creative Music

Re-creative music is the artistic performance of the work of another. Notes can be read correctly as a mathematical problem, yet performed unmusically. A song should be interpreted artistically, giving the listener the mood, the beauty of melodic line, the harmony or the rhythm intended. An instrumental number should be re-created artistically on the melody bells, the tonette, the piano, or other instrument.

Some people fear that attention to dynamics (loud and soft), tempo (speed), and phrasing will spoil the music for the children. Such fears are ungrounded unless interpretation is a matter of drill. If interpretation is drawn from the children, it makes the music appealing and beautiful. If music is not a beautiful experience, it has lost its reason for existence. Approached democratically, children find great satisfaction in an aesthetic experience.

Creative Music

Creative music originates with the creator. Children may create songs, rhythmic activities, instruments, or ways to use instruments. Beginning efforts may seem crude, but creativity comes from creating. The teacher herself may feel awkward in initiating attempts along creative lines, but she will soon find the children becoming more and more responsive.

Most teachers inhibit creativity rather than foster and nurture it. Unconsciously they try to make children conform to the more common rhythms and tonalities. Is there any particular reason why a song should end on the keynote? Why should songs sung in the minor mode be changed to major? Young children quite often create their songs in the minor mode, or in the pentatonic scale. Children will conform soon enough when they have more experience. Truly great composers are those who found new ways to express themselves.

¶ WHAT CAN CREATIVE MUSIC DO FOR THE CHILD?

Creative experiences can
1. Offer a child the opportunity to do something truly his own in which he is not compelled to conform.
2. Help develop powers of observation, discrimination, and judgment in the child.
3. Give the child further opportunity to cooperate with the group.
4. Provide an aesthetic experience.
5. Encourage originality.

Creative Rhythmic Activities

¶ CREATIVE RHYTHMIC INTERPRETATION OF MUSIC — This activity may take the form of free movement. That is, a composition may be played and the children encouraged to interpret freely what they hear. They may become fairies, goblins, airplanes or elephants. They may just move as they wish without "being" anything in particular. They may create designs on the floor. They may act out entire stories. They should be encouraged to tell what in the music made them think certain things were happening. (Chapter V.) After children have given their own ideas of the music, the teacher may or may not tell them the original intent of the composer. The class may wish to interpret his ideas.

¶ CREATIVE DANCE — Children may analyze the music by phrases and create their own dances (see p. 26), or they may create their dances spontaneously as they listen to the music.

¶ CREATIVE RHYTHMS — In this activity the children develop

*Rattle
dance*

Creative dance

bodily sequences to interpret what they see, feel, or think. This is done *independently* of any music. For example, suppose the class has been to the dairy. One group developed the following sequence:

Activities	*Accompaniment*
Cows in the pasture	
Walking slowly	drum
Grazing	pompons
Drinking	castanets
Cows herded into the barn	
Walking faster	coconuts
Cows enter stanchions and are fed	
Switching tails	pompons
Eating	wire drum stick on drum
Cows are washed	sand blocks

Egyptian frieze

Creative rhythms

Emotion in bodily expression   *"Jabberwocky," by Lewis Carroll*

Cows are milked   tambourine, shaken delicately for sound of milk hitting side of pail

Some of the children were cows, some herdsmen, some formed the stanchions. Others fed the cows. Then some washed the imaginary udders and finally placed the imaginary stools and milked the cows.

Children worked in groups planning each rhythmic activity before performing it for the class. Then the class gave suggestions. It is extremely important that the children do the planning. Care must be exercised in order that the result is not mere dramatization. This is creative *rhythm*. The teacher made a tagboard chart of the sequences to facilitate later duplication of the activity with the children exchanging parts. The sound effects were selected by suggestion, trial, and error. Cow faces painted by the children on brown paper sacks made the second performance more realistic.

One child expressed the wish that they had real music to accompany the rhythms. The teacher suggested that some of the class listen to recordings to locate something suitable. A committee of volunteers listened to many recordings and then presented *Norwegian Dance No. 2* by Grieg. By replaying the last theme, this music fit perfectly. The fast part corresponded with the hurrying of the cattle into the barn. The committee had listened intelligently to many records and had noted some they wanted to hear again later.

The teacher capitalized upon the selection of *Norwegian Dance No. 2* and told the class that Grieg had lived in farm country. The class wanted to know more about him, and one boy volunteered to read and report. He became the class authority on Grieg.

Another day, some of the class were milk bottles conveyed on an imaginary belt in columns of two to the washing vat where they were dunked, then filled and capped. They used a short shuffling step as they were "conveyed on the belt." The "man" bent each child from the waist to dunk him in the vat. Then the bottles shuffled on to be filled, capped and placed in carriers. Sound effects were added.

The two preceding creative rhythms show how children can interpret things, both animate and inanimate.

Creative Use of Instruments

Instruments were used creatively in the preceding activities. Selections may be made simultaneously as each sequence is created, or they may be added after the entire rhythmic activity is finished. A good teacher avoids routine and varies the approach in creative notation. They may then be written on tagboard, decorated by the experiences.

Instruments may also be used to enrich songs. One class used wood blocks for the sound of wooden shoes, and swishing pompons for the turning windmills in a little Dutch song. A realistic youngster squeaked the lid of the piano bench. He had been to Holland and remembered the creaking sound of the windmills.

Maracas, guiros, castanets, claves and drums lend atmosphere to songs of Mexico and South America. Children should first be encouraged to try these instruments as they wish. Some will capture the Latin-American flavor at once. If help is *needed,* the teacher may encourage a continuous double rhythm with the maracas, ♪♪ ♪♪ ♪♪ ♪♪ A simple technique for acquiring an almost authentic clave rhythm may be developed by having the children chant   Shave, hair cut, six bits as they play (See p. 165 for instructions for holding the claves.)

Instruments should be used with good taste, and not allowed to overbalance the singing. Evaluation by the children themselves helps increase their powers of discrimination.

Making Songs

There are many ways of making songs in class. Several procedures will be suggested here, but the teacher should not be afraid to experiment for different ways and to evolve a plan of her own which will be easiest for her.

Singing conversations (see p. 83) are the simplest introduction to making songs. Some of these conversations may develop into songs and may be written down by the teacher in line or standard notation, and displayed in the classroom. The following grew from a discussion about a little calf which the first graders° had watched.

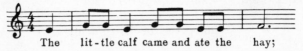

The   lit - tle calf came and ate the   hay;

° Songs created by first and second grades, Cortez Elementary School, Los Angeles, California, Beatrice Grosbayne, teacher.

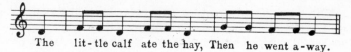

The lit-tle calf ate the hay, Then he went a-way.

This group also made a song about their pet hamster.

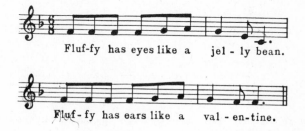

Fluf-fy has eyes like a jel-ly bean.

Fluf-fy has ears like a val-en-tine.

Words and music may be created simultaneously, or the words may be created first, then set to music. One teacher asks the entire class to sing softly the words they have created beforehand. She moves about among the singers jotting down the tunes she hears. Then, using her notes, she sings the different phrases to the class, and the children select the music they consider most suitable. Extreme tact must be exercised at all times in music classes, but especially during *creative* music. A child belittled or ignored will seldom volunteer again. Strangely, a poor singer may contribute a truly lovely phrase of his own. Inability to repeat the music of another is no indication that a person cannot create music of his own. Recognition of such a contribution by a child may be the opening wedge for his entrance into other musical activities.

Another teacher asks for volunteers to sing a melody for each phrase of a poem previously written. The class evaluates these melodies and selects the ones they consider most suitable. Sometimes they combine the first part of the efforts of one child with the last of the efforts of another. Or sometimes they change some of the melodies slightly. For example, in one song about swinging high, the children changed the music to make it go high. The teacher should encourage intelligent discrimination without dictating her own ideas. Care must be exercised in order that one or two children do not monopolize the song during class composition. There are always a few who will create entire songs at a moment's notice. They should be encouraged to do this at other times, but to share the experience with others during class time.

A third grade teacher writes the words of the song on the chalk-board. As different members of the class sing the phrases, she records them on notepaper. Then the class as a whole decides which phrases to use. As they sing the song, they indicate the pitch levels with their hands. This is then recorded above the words on the chalk-board.

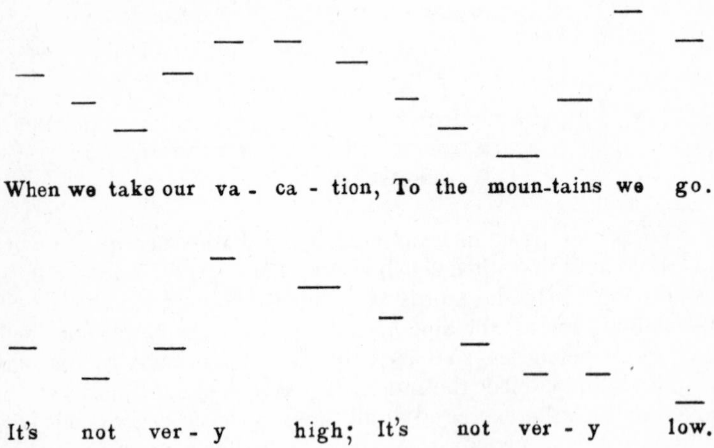

When we take our va - ca - tion, To the moun-tains we go.

It's not ver - y high; It's not ver - y low.

This may be the extent of the work for one day; or, the extent of the ability of a particular group.

The children then locate the accents and place the measure bars before the accented words or syllables. If the song swings in 3's, they place the figure 3 before the song.

Individual children may step the rhythmic pattern of the melody of the various phrases as the rest of the class claps. (Use of the whole body in stepping seems to clarify line lengths better than clapping.) When a child has stepped a phrase, he may change the line notation to rhythmic line notation.

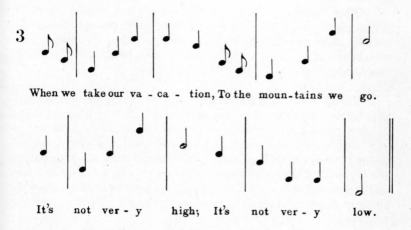

When we take our va - ca - tion, To the moun-tains we go.

It's not ver - y high; It's not ver - y low.

Sometimes the children change the line notation to standard notation at this point, and sometimes they do so after the staff has been added.

3

When we take our va - ca - tion, To the moun-tains we go.

It's not ver - y high; It's not ver - y low.

The teacher then draws the lines of the staff over the preceding notation, and has approximately° this:

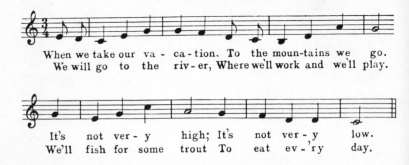

When we take our va - ca - tion, To the moun-tains we go.
We will go to the riv - er, Where we'll work and we'll play.

It's not ver - y high; It's not ver - y low.
We'll fish for some trout To eat ev - 'ry day.

Playing the song on the melody bells or the piano reveals any errors. Clef signs, the lower figure, title and other verses are added.

Some teachers place the initial note of the song on the staff and help the children to place the other notes, utilizing familiar tonal patterns.

Other teachers start with the rhythm of the words. Then the melody is created to fit the rhythm. Sometimes, however, when the melody is composed, the rhythm is changed. For this reason time may be saved by composing the melody and the rhythm simultaneously.

¶ SUGGESTIONS FOR NOTATING A SONG — Songs will warrant display in the classroom. For this purpose a staff liner made of strips of screen molding about one inch wide tacked to strips of lath is very useful. (See figure 1.) Sanding the wood and waxing or varnishing it will prevent splinters in the hands. Lay the liner flat on the tagboard and use a Flowmaster pen or a crayon to draw a line above each slat of the liner. Some teachers prefer a liner with twenty strips of molding. This will serve as a guide for four staves on the tagboard.

If a flannel board is used, staff lines may be made of masking tape, or string, or they may be painted on the flannel. Commercially made flannel boards with staffs may be purchased.

° This song was created by a third grade in the Garvanza School, Los Angeles, California, teacher, Mrs. Dorothy Woolsey.

Figure 1

Figure 1

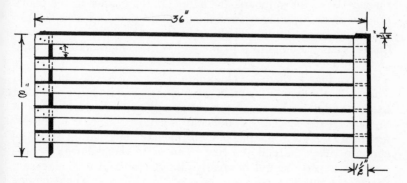

Children's songs are generally notated according to phrases, that is, one phrase to a staff. Each staff should be the same length as the others. It may be necessary to crowd some phrases and to spread others in order to make the staves even on the tagboard. Manila tagboard is suitable and is available in most schools. Rolls of large staff paper (newspaper weight) may be purchased.

It is wise to write the song first on staff paper as a plan. The clef sign, the key signature and the meter signature (in that order) should be included at the beginning of the song. The clef sign and the key signature should be placed at the beginning of *each* staff. The meter signature appears *only* on the *first* staff (unless the meter changes within the song). The third line of the staff is the center, and the stems of all note heads above the center generally turn *down*. Those below the third line turn *up*. Those on the third line may turn either way. Stems turning up are placed on the *right* of the note head. Those turning down are placed on the *left* of the note head.

Measure bars should precede the accents of the words. (See p. 27.) If a staff ends on an incomplete measure, the measure bar is omitted. A double bar is used at the end of the song. A ruler or other straight object used to make the note stems and the measure bars gives the song a neat appearance. If an error is made, a piece of matching paper or tagboard may be pasted over the error and the correction made on top of the new piece. Sometimes a bit of decoration strategically placed will conceal a blot or other error. Children enjoy decorating the tagboard around the song. Upper grade students can notate their own songs on the tagboard. More experienced children may also notate harmony parts and number the chords for the autoharp, the harmolin, the ukelele or the piano. For the words, printing with an almost professional appearance may be attained by the use of circles and lines. The circles may be traced around a dime or a penny and vertical lines added to complete the letters.

Occasionally there is a child in the class who has absolute pitch. That is, he can notate the exact pitch of any tone he hears. An alert teacher will capitalize upon this talent and allow the child to use it in class. If the teacher has difficulty notating a song, it is entirely permissible to go to the piano or the melody bells and pick out "by ear" the tunes the children sing, then write them down. A tape recorder is very helpful in creative music. This gives the teacher the opportunity to record the songs of the children. Then she can notate them later from the tape.

Composing Music for Words Already Written

One third grade class° was preparing a Christmas program. They wanted to sing " 'Twas the Night Before Christmas," but published arrangements were too difficult for them. They therefore decided to make their own musical arrangement for this old favorite poem.

First they learned the poem for choral speaking. Then they set parts of it to music of their own creation. A child with absolute pitch notated the music on the chalkboard. The class selected suitable rhythm instruments for sound effects. One child played a theme from *The Nutcracker Suite* by Tchaikovsky on the melody bells as the class recited ". . . and visions of sugarplums danced o'er his head." (This theme, of course, was from the "Dance of the Sugarplum Fairy.") Finally a talented child went to the piano and played a simple chord accompaniment for the singing parts. The finished product was their own, and the children, their teacher and their parents enjoyed it.

Making Instruments

Children enjoy making simple instruments which may be used for song enrichment, accompaniment for rhythmic activities, or ac-

---

° Hutton School, Spokane, Washington, teacher, Miss Gretchen Stieler.

companiment to music heard. Of course, young children cannot make the more complicated instruments. If the school does not furnish these, they may be made by upper grade students or by the parents.

One teacher asked her room parents to come to school during the evenings and make instruments. The project was interesting to the parents and also served as a means of developing friendship among the parents, friendship between parents and the teacher, and interest in the school. When the instruments were finished, the parents visited school to see them in use. Needless to say, they found ways to secure much other needed equipment, including a good phonograph and a fine collection of records.

In another school a scout troop which had made drums for their own use decided to do a good turn for the younger children. They made a collection of rhythm instruments for the school.

SUGGESTIONS FOR MAKING INSTRUMENTS

A. JINGLES AND RINGS

1. *Bells*
   a. Use bicycle bells.
   b. Use door bells.
   c. Buy small jingle bells at the dime stores. (These are available during the Christmas season.) Sew to strips of tape or ribbon and tie to ankles or wrists. These are very effective with some Christmas songs.
   d. Attach parakeet bells to sticks.
   e. Aluminum gelatin molds, *if* they have a good tone quality, may be used. Drill a hole in the bottom of each. Tie a large knot in the end of a heavy cord. Draw the other end of the cord through the hole in one of the molds. About four inches above this, tie another knot and add another mold. Add a third above this. Strike with a small nail.

2. *Triangles*
   a. Heat a steel rod or a curtain rod and bend into the shape of a triangle leaving an open space at the end. Heating at the corners will temporarily destroy the tone quality. This will be restored by heating each side of the triangle and immediately dipping it in cold water. Strike with a small rod or a nail.
   b. Suspend a long nail, a bolt or a horseshoe from a string or a thong. Strike with a small nail.

3. *Tambourines*
   a. Cover wooden embroidery hoops with Bohemian or down ticking. Staple cloth in place with staples very close together. Paint the cloth with airplane or nitrate dope. (This is available at hobby shops and

hardware stores.) Use four or five coats and allow each coat to dry thoroughly before adding another. Fasten roofing tins or flattened bottle caps to the hoops.

    b. Attach flattened bottle caps or roofing tins to the edge of a paper plate. Decorate the plate with paint. Two plates may be laced together before the tins are attached. (Cork should be removed from bottle caps.)

    c. Attach tiny sleigh bells to hoops or plates. Tambourines may be held in the right hand and struck on the left hand, elbow, or knee, or they may be shaken.

4. *Indian Rain Rattles*

    a. Fashion cones from segments of roofing tins, flattened bottle caps or circles cut from tin cans. These cones may be shaped over the sharpened end of a piece of doweling. Cones of different sizes give a variety of tones. The handle may be a flat piece of wood or a piece of one-inch doweling. Drill about ten holes along the side of this handle at intervals of about three-quarters of an inch. Cut colored cord or thong into ten eight-inch lengths. Knot one end of each cord and pass the other end through a cone and then a hole in the handle. Knot both strands together close to the handle, then pass the loose end of the cord through another cone and tie a knot. This will make a double row of ten cones each.
Play by shaking.

    b. Substitute tiny Christmas bells for the cones. These do not give the Indian effect, but are useful for other sound effects.

B. SHAKERS.

1. *Rattles*

    a. Place a *few tiny* pebbles, seeds, beads, rice, or fine shot in small boxes. Seal with glue or tape. Small food cartons make good shakers. Wax can be removed by wiping with a cloth dipped in vinegar or gasoline; then the cartons may be painted. Handles may be made of pieces of doweling passed through the bottom of the box and tacked to the top. About one-half teaspoonful of fine shot or rice makes a good sound. Avoid using too much, or material that is too heavy.

2. *Maracas*

    a. Latin-American type

Select small gourds with handles. Gourds must be ripe and dry. Soak the gourds in water, then scrub using steel wool if necessary. Allow to dry thoroughly before beginning work. Sand the gourd until it is smooth.

If the seeds already give a satisfactory rattle, it is not necessary to open the gourd. Otherwise, pencil a line on the gourd perpendicular to the intended saw-cut. Use a hack saw lightly to cut completely through. Too much pressure will crush the gourd.

Fill the handle with small pieces of paper mixed with airplane or nitrate dope, or shellac. Allow to dry. Matching the pencil marks, cement the gourd back together. Cracks may be filled with wood putty. Sand, decorate, and shellac.

*Latin-American
instruments.
Left to right,
Maracas
Guiro
Cabaca
Claves*

Round gourds may be used by adding a handle of doweling. Open the gourd and remove the pulp and seeds. Drive a large headed tack through the bottom of the gourd into a six-inch length of doweling. Glue a card or a piece of parchment paper over the open end of the lower half of the gourd. Place the shot in the top half and cement the two halves of the gourd together. The paper membrane keeps the shot in the end of the gourd and produces a better sound. Smooth with sandpaper, decorate and shellac.

Latin-American maracas are used in pairs. One should have a sharper sound than the other.

Play by grasping a handle in each hand and shaking the gourds alternately.

b. Hawaiian gourds (*Uliuli*)

Plastic clothes sprinklers make good Hawaiian shakers. Heat a darning needle, insert it through a hole into the cork of the sprinkler top; then immediately after withdrawing it, insert a small colored feather in the hole. When the plastic cools, the feather will be held securely. Place a feather in each hole of the sprinkler top. Suitable feathers may be purchased at headquarters for Scouts and Campfire Girls. Place a few grains of rice or fine shot in the container end of the sprinkler and insert the feathered cork.

Hawaiian gourds are played by grasping one with the right hand just below the feathers, smacking the other end against the palm of the left hand on the strong beats, and shaking it on the weak beats.

3. *Seed Pods* (Indian)

Monkey tree pods, jacaranda pods and eucalyptus pods may be used. Fasten them to doweling or attach to anklets or bracelets to wear while dancing.

4. *Cabaça* (pronounced ka-bah'sa) (Latin-American)

a. Gourd type

Scrub and sandpaper a large, handled gourd. Mark and saw in two. Remove pulp, add one-half teaspoonful of shot, and cement together again. Paint and loosely string with large wooden beads on heavy cord or raffia.

b. Coconut cabaça

Drill a hole in one eye and drain the milk. Mark the coconut perpendicularly and saw in two with a cross-cut saw. Remove the meat. Plug the hole drilled for draining, or cover with masking tape. Cut a hole for the handle in one end; match the marks and cement the coconut back together. Sandpaper lightly, but leave slightly rough. Paint or shellac. Pour about one-half teaspoonful of fine shot into the hole and insert the handle. Doweling may be used. The part which fits inside the coconut should be trimmed down in order that the thicker part will fit snugly against the coconut to keep the shot inside. Drive a large headed nail through the end of the coconut into the end of the handle which is inside the coconut. Make a mesh of wire with large beads or coffee beans. This should fit over the coconut, but not be wired into a stationary position. This mesh is held in the left hand while the right hand twists the handle. This scrapes the coconut against the beads on the mesh.

C. STROKERS

1. *Sand Blocks*

Attach handles to blocks of wood about three-quarters of an inch thick. (Make certain that nails or screws do not protrude through the bottom of the block as they will wear through the sandpaper.)

Paint or shellac. Cover the flat surface with sandpaper or garnet paper. (Different grained papers give different sounds. Variety is desirable.) Gluing the paper to the block destroys the tone quality and makes replacement difficult when the sand is worn off. It is better to fold the paper over the sides and tack to the top of the block with thumbtacks, being careful to keep them away from the playing surface.

Long nine-inch sand blocks are better for some sound effects.

Play by stroking the sandpaper surfaces together.

2. *Grooved Sticks*

File grooves close together around dowel sticks.

Play by stroking one stick across the other.

3. *Moraches* (Indian)

Cut notches in a stick. Stroke with another plain stick. The Indians placed the end of the notched stick against a hollow gourd for resonance. (An interesting scientific principle.)

4. *Guiro* (pronounced wee-ro) (Latin-American)

Select a gourd about fourteen to eighteen inches long. Choose one with a thick solid shell. Scrub and sandpaper. In the side of the large end, slightly below the middle, drill a hole large enough for the thumb. File and sand the edges smooth. Using a bent wire (a coat hanger will do) pull the dry pulp out of the gourd. File deep horizontal grooves on the surface, close together on the side opposite the thumb hole. Use a half round and/or a triangular file. Decorate and shellac, leaving the grooved portion natural for better tone quality.

Hold by inserting the left thumb in the hole, and play by stroking the grooves with a pocket-comb or a thin piece of doweling. A stroker may be made by inserting three or four short prongs of heavy wire (such as that in an old coat hanger) into a small piece of wood.

D. CLICKS

1. *Wood Blocks*
   a. Attach a handle to a small wooden block.
      Play by striking with a mallet.
   b. Make a smooth wood block about five inches by two and one-half inches and two inches thick. Glue thin strips of wood across three sides of one of the large surfaces. Attach a five-inch by two and one-half-inch by one-quarter-inch piece of wood to cover the strips. This will form a hollow center to the block. Sandpaper. File the edges to a smooth rounding surface and sand the entire block. Paint with shellac or lacquer.
      Play by striking with a mallet. Striking different parts of the block gives different pitches and tone quality. Holding the block in the cupped left hand adds resonance. Different sized blocks give variety in pitch.
   c. Make a mallet by inserting a twelve-inch length of small doweling into a wooden ball or a large wooden bead. A one-half-inch piece of one-inch doweling may be tacked through the center to a small doweling handle and used as a mallet.

2. *Sticks*
   a. Use doweling of different sizes. Paint or shellac varies the sound.
   b. Use bamboo.
   c. Chopsticks make good sticks.
   d. Rungs from old chairs may also be used.

3. *Claves* (pronounced kläh'vāz) (Latin-American)

Cut broomsticks or hardwood doweling into six-inch lengths. Sand and shellac.

Play by holding one stick in the cupped left hand and striking with the other stick grasped in the right hand. The cup forms a resonating chamber.

4. *Wooden Salad Bowl*

Drill two holes in the edge of the bowl and suspend from a heavy cord or thong handle; or cord may be attached by heavy staples in the edge of the bowl. Decorate and shellac.

Play by striking with a mallet. Striking the bowl in different places gives different sounds.

5. *Coconut Shells*

   Drill a hole in one of the eyes and drain the milk. Saw in two using a cross-cut saw. Remove the meat. Dry thoroughly. Sand and shellac.

   Play by holding one half in each hand and clapping them together. Coconuts are especially good for imitating the sound of horses' hoofs.

6. *Castanets*

   Hollow out an English walnut. Place a tongue-depressor between the two halves of the nut and attach all three together at one end of the nut. When the handle is shaken, the halves of the nut will click against the depressor. Seashells may be used in place of the nut shells. Fasten small seashells together in pairs like commercial castanets. Loop the cords over the thumbs and play as commercial castanets.

   Ili-ili (pronounced ee-lee) (Hawaiian)

   Select four small round flat rocks. Hold one between the thumb and the forefinger of each hand. Click these against the other two which are resting lightly against the pads of the other three fingers of each hand.

E. DRUMS

1. *Carton Drums*

   Ice cream containers, gaily decorated, are satisfactory drums for some activities. Small children can decorate them. (Remove wax with vinegar or gasoline before painting.) Beat on the bottom of the carton. Cereal boxes can be used for drums. Some of them have a fair tone. They may be decorated by the children. Play with the hands or a beater.

2. *Wooden Drums*

   Use nail kegs, candy buckets, butter tubs, wine kegs, barrels, or large wooden salad bowls. Sand the wood surface, remove the top and drill a large hole in the bottom. Generally speaking, the larger the air chamber, the deeper the tone. However, the material and the tautness of the drum head also affect the tone.

   Drum heads may be made from inner tubes or live rubber, Bohemian or down ticking, parchment paper, or old discarded drum heads. Live rubber may be purchased at hobby shops, ticking at dry goods departments, and discarded or new drum heads at instrument repair shops. Be sure that the edges of the drum are smooth before attaching the drum head. Heads may be tacked on wooden kegs or buckets or salad bowls. Tack opposite sides while pulling the material firmly. Thumb-tacks or upholstery tacks are suitable. Place them *very* close together to prevent later loosening. If ticking is used, first brush a band of air-plane or nitrate dope around the edge of the taut drum head. When thoroughly dry, apply a coat of dope over the entire surface, drawing all brush strokes in the same direction. Apply five to eight coats of dope, allowing each to dry thoroughly before adding the next, and brushing each in the opposite direction from the last. Airplane or nitrate dope may be purchased at hobby shops and hardware stores. Clear dope seems to give a better tone than some of the colored dopes.

   If a skin head is used, soak it in water at room temperature for about thirty minutes. Squeeze out the water and stretch it over the top of the drum. Tack in the same manner as explained for a cloth head.

Drums

KEG	GOURD	HEAVY CARTON
Double headed	*Down ticking*	*Double headed*
Down ticking heads		*Skin laced*
BARREL	RATTLE DRUM	PAPIER-MACHÉ
Double headed	*Coconut with*	VEGETABLE BASKET
Inner tube laced	*pebbles inside*	*Down ticking*
	Skin laced	

Allow to dry thoroughly before touching. Unsightly tack heads may be brushed with glue and covered with felt, or by winding heavy cotton rope around the drum over the tack heads.

If a skin head becomes loose, place the drum in the sun, on a slightly warm radiator, or in a slightly warm oven for a time. It may tighten.

3. *Metal Drums*

If a metal pail or oil drum is used, draw the head taut and hold in place by wrapping a wire or wet leather thong tightly around the drum just under the upper edge of the drum. If the head is of ticking, paint it with dope. If it is skin, soak it before applying it. Be sure to have a hole in the bottom of the container, to prevent a metallic rattle and to amplify the tone.

4. *Flowerpot Drums*

Fasten the head in the same manner as for a metal drum, using a wire or a leather thong under the edge of the collar of the pot.

5. *Double Headed Drums*

Remove both top and bottom of keg, barrel or can. Use soaked skin head or strong rubber. Lace the two heads together with a wet leather thong drawn tightly. If rubber is used, extra thickness vulcanized over the strategic spots before punching the holes may prevent tearing.

6. *Gourd Drum*

Select a large solid gourd. Scrub, dry and sand smooth. Saw off the large end. Remove the pulp and seeds. Sand the edges smooth. Staple down ticking over the open end, making sure to place the staples close together. Brush a band of dope around the edge of the ticking and proceed as with any other cloth head. Cover staples with glue and attach cotton rope to cover them. Decorate. If there is a handle to the gourd, attach a long rope braid to the band of rope and to the handle of the gourd. This is used to hang the drum around the neck and over the shoulder of the player.

Play with the hands or a beater.

7. *Finger Drums*

a. Make a gourd drum using a small, handled gourd. Use wet parchment paper for the head. Tack on with colored thumbtacks. Do not strike until thoroughly dry.

b. Use a small wooden salad bowl. Attach a doorstop to the center of the bottom of the bowl. Use down ticking, skin, or parchment paper for the head.

Hold the drum by grasping the doorstop with the left hand. Play using the fingers of the right hand.

c. Bongo drums. Make two small drums of different sizes and fasten them together. Hold between the knees and play with the fingers of both hands.

8. *Conga Drum* (Latin-American)

Use a deep barrel with a skin head. Elk's hide makes a good head. Apply wet.

9. *Tumbaita* (Latin-American)

Take a deep barrel apart and taper each stave toward the bottom. Fasten the staves together again with heavy wire hoops. This makes a deep, conical drum. Use a skin head. Leave the small bottom open. Attach a wide heavy leather strap for the player to wear over his shoulder to hold the drum in place. Play with the hands.

10. *Drum Beaters*

a. Insert and glue a piece of one-half-inch doweling into a hole drilled in a small wooden ball whittled from a block of wood, or a spool with the rims whittled down even with the center. The head may be covered with cloth, felt or chamois.

b. Insert a dowel into a firm rubber ball.

c. Insert and glue a dowel into a fishnet cork ball.

d. Use the heel of a shoe tree. This may be covered with cloth, felt or chamois.

F. GONGS

Some frying pans, cake pans, pie pans, kettles, and brass plates make good gongs. Suspend them with cord, thong, yarn or other material. Experiment to find the best material for this. (Paint deadens the tone of metal.)

G. POMPONS or SWISHERS

Use one (or two) packages of crepe paper. Cut a one-inch strip from one end of the package. Shred the package into strips one inch wide, leaving five inches on one edge uncut. Open the package, then roll the uncut edge tightly together. Wind the one-inch strip tightly around the roll over the uncut portion. Cover with Scotch tape. This forms a handle of the paper itself. If preferred, the uncut portion of the paper may be wound around a piece of doweling, tacked and covered with crepe paper or Scotch tape.

H. HAWAIIAN PUILI STICKS (pronounced poo-ee'lee)

Use bamboo about twenty inches long and one and one-half inches across. The joint should be near one end. Be sure the bamboo is dry. About three and one-half inches below the joint, drill holes about three-eighths of an inch apart around the bamboo. Slit the bamboo from the free end to each hole. Pare each shred a little to separate the shreds. (The drilled holes prevent the bamboo from splitting the entire length.)

Hold the thick joint end of the bamboo in the right hand, and play by tapping the slit end on the palm of the left hand, the back of the hand, the floor, the shoulder, the knee, or against the bamboo of another player. Children will enjoy experimenting for effects. These bamboos are used for rhythmic accompaniment in Hawaii.

Hawaiian Luau (note puili sticks)

I. XYLOPHONES (Making these requires a keen ear.)

1. *Bottle Xylophones*

Select large bottles or jars with good tones. Add varying amounts of water and arrange according to the major scale. Add or subtract water to each bottle until the scale is complete. Mark the water levels with nail polish or adhesive tape, and label the bottles 1 — 8, do — do, or with the letter names of the pitches. Ink, vegetable dye or crepe paper may be used to color the water. Appoint children to keep the water at the correct levels. Replacement of caps or corks will prevent rapid evaporation, but may affect the tone quality. Have the children experiment to select the best material to use under the bottles (felt, paper, wood, glass). Bottles may be suspended.

Strike with chopsticks or mallets (p. 165).

2. *Glass Xylophones*

Test glasses for pitch and tone quality. Arrange in order of the scale. Label. Add colored water when necessary. Experiment with sound when placed on cloth, paper, felt, or rubber cushions and on hard surfaces.

Glasses or bottles of the correct pitch without addition of water save work in upkeep, but are more difficult to locate.

A tray may be made to keep bottles or glasses in order. Arrange glasses on a smooth piece of plywood. Mark around the bottom of each glass and cut a circle in the plywood the exact size of each glass. Glue or nail the plywood with the holes to another piece of wood of the same size. (Place a piece of flannel or felt between the two pieces of wood for a cushion for the glasses.) Attach a handle to each end of the tray to simplify carrying. Place the glasses in their respective places.

Strike glasses with chopsticks, small dowels or mallets.

3. *Wood Xylophones*

California redwood is resonant and easy to use. Basswood, poplar and whitewood are also suitable. About fifteen feet of wood one and one-half inches wide and one-half to five-eighths inches thick will be needed. Saw off a piece of wood nine inches long. Strike it, matching the tone with the piano, bells, or a pitch-pipe. Cut the next piece one-half inch shorter. Test with the second tone of the scale. If the pitch is too low, shave or sand a little off the end. If it is too high, sand a little off the surface of the bar. Continue the same way for the other pitches. Remember that the half steps occur between the 3rd and 4th and the 7th and 8th tones of the major scale. It is easier to hear the pitch if the bars are placed over an open box while testing.

Locate the nodal points (places where there is the least vibration). Each nodal point will be a little less than one-fourth of the length from the end of the bar. Place a few grains of sand on the bar and strike it in several places. The sand will collect at the nodal point.

Nail the bars to rope at the nodal points, using small nails or carpet tacks; or construct a small frame on which the bars may be laid. The top of the frame should be cushioned with rope, a strip of felt, a strip of windshield wiper rubber or weatherstripping. This makes the bars more resonant.

Paint the numbers or letters on the bars, and wax.

Mallets may be made from quarter-inch doweling attached to small balls whittled from wood, or to quarter-inch circles cut from five-eighths-inch doweling, or to large wooden beads.

J. CHIMES (These also require a keen ear.)

1. *Tuned Nails*

Purchase long nails or bolts with a good tone quality. Six inches is a good length.

Use the piano, melody bells or a pitch pipe to determine the pitch of one of the nails. (If they are all the same kind, they will be about the same pitch.)

Use a hack saw to cut off about one-quarter inch of another nail. Test and use a file to adjust the pitch. Suspend the nails from strings when testing. Strike with another nail.

Tune the others the same way, remembering the half steps between 3 and 4 and 7 and 8 in the diatonic major scale.

If the starting nail is "so" or 5, the scale to high "mi" or 3 is possible. Suspend the nails by string from cup hooks on a wooden standard, being careful to keep the nails far enough apart to prevent them from jingling together when struck.

Strike with another nail.

2. *Flowerpot Chimes*

The flowerpots must be selected for their pitch, as little can be done to adjust the pitch. Be sure the pots are clean and dry when testing. Suspend each pot from a rack by means of a cord passed through the hole in the bottom of the pot, through a button, and back through the hole in the pot. The button keeps the cord from pulling off the pot.

A rack similar to the one for nails is suitable, but it must be large enough to keep the flowerpots apart when they are struck.

Clay flowerpots absorb moisture and may change in pitch during damp weather. This makes a good lesson in science.

Strike with a hard mallet.

3. *Tubular Chimes*

Use aluminum or brass tubing. Drill two holes opposite each other in the top of each pipe. Suspend each pipe by a hard cord. (Holes must be drilled *before* tuning.) Cut tubes with a hack saw, beginning with a tube about nineteen and one-half inches long. Shorten the next tube about one inch. Continue up the scale, testing often and remembering that the half steps fall between 3 and 4, and 7 and 8 in the major scale. Use a file to raise the pitch. A very little filing will alter the pitch.

Polish the pipes with steel wool.

Pipes should be hung from a frame, far enough apart so that they will not touch each other when struck. Letter or number names of the pitches may be marked on the rod from which the pipes are suspended. Marking the pipes themselves may affect the tone quality.

Making any instrument with pitch requires a keen ear. It is valuable in causing students to be aware of pitch, but if the instruments are not in tune, they should *not* be used in the classroom, except for sound effects not requiring definite pitch. Poorly tuned instruments tend to deaden the pitch acuity of children, and do more harm than good. However, some persons are able to make instruments which are in better tune than some commercial instruments. (Commercial instruments should be tested by a qualified person before purchase and not accepted if out-of-tune.)

Any suggestions for playing the above instruments are for the teacher. Children should be allowed to experiment and to find interesting ways to play. However, there are times when the teacher may wish to guide the children.

One teacher° constructed a rack for keeping the class rhythm instruments in place. It was an attractive piece of furniture with hooks and spaces for all equipment. The children were proud of their instruments and kept them in order. The teacher felt that the very fact that the instruments were always in sight and easily accessible, contributed to spontaneity and creativeness.

Experimentation reveals many new and interesting ways of creating instruments. The teacher should be alert at all times for new ideas. Since this chapter was started, an excellent drum was made of papier-mâché. Strips of the paper were glued over a cheap vegetable basket. A head of down ticking was added. The tone surpassed many of the more common types of drums. Do not be afraid to try new ideas.

Questions for Class Discussion

1. What forms may creative music take in the elementary school? Can you think of some not mentioned in this chapter?
2. How could creative music contribute to other subjects in the elementary school?
3. How could you make the parents aware of the creative musical activities in your classroom?
4. Which of the creative projects studied in the foregoing chapter do you feel you could carry on most successfully? (Your answer will depend a great deal upon your musical background.)

° Mrs. Margaret Kester, La Canada, California Elementary Schools.

Suggested Assignments

1. Write a song of your own, keeping in mind the fact that the music should fit the rhythm of the words.
2. Put your song on tagboard for classroom display, as you would a song your class had created.
3. Make some instrument which you can use to advantage when you start teaching. Write the description of your work in such a way that another could follow your directions. Mention any difficulties encountered, and tell how they could be avoided.

General References

ACEI Committee, "We Make Our Own," *Childhood Education* 30:329-31 54.

Adams, Fay, *Educating America's Children*. New York: Ronald Press, 1946, pp. 408-412.

Andrews, Gladys, *Creative Rhythmic Movement for Children*. New York: Prentice-Hall, Inc., 1954.

Cole, Natalie, *The Arts in the Classroom*. New York: John Day Co., Inc., 1940.

*Coleman, Satis, *The Book of Bells*. New York: John Day Co., Inc., 1938.

Coleman, Satis, *First Steps in Playing and Composing*. New York: John Day Co., Inc., 1930.

Coleman, Satis, *The Marimba Book*. New York: John Day Co., Inc., 1930.

Dykema, Peter W. and Cundiff, Hannah M., *School Music Handbook*. Boston: C. C. Birchard & Co., 1955, pp. 52-57, 120-121, 218-232, 541-544, 560-564.

Fitzsimmons, Grace, "Why Not Make Musical Instruments?" *School Arts* 51:-246, 247. March 52.

*Fox, Lillian Mohr and Hopkins, L. Thomas, *Creative School Music*. New York: Silver Burdett Co., 1936.

*Griswold, Lester, *Handicraft*. Colorado: Out West Printing and Stationery Co., 1942, pp. 147, 445-446.

Heffernan, Helen et al, *Guiding the Young Child*. Boston: D. C. Heath & Co., 1951, Ch. X.

Hood, Marguerite and Schultz, Ernest J., *Learning Music Through Rhythm*. Boston: Ginn & Co., 1949, Ch. XIII.

Krone, Beatrice Perham, *Music in the New School*. Chicago: Neil A. Kjos Music Co., Revised 1947, Ch. V.

Lee, J. Murray and Lee, Dorris May, *The Child and His Curriculum*. New York: Appleton-Century-Crofts, Inc., 1950, pp. 606-607, 636-639.

Mace, Katherine, *Let's Dance a Story*. New York: Abelard-Schuman, Inc., 1955.

Mason, Bernard S., *Drums, Tom-toms and Rattles*. New York: A. S. Barnes & Co., 1938.

Mathews, Paul Wentworth, *You Can Teach Music*. New York: E. P. Dutton & Co., Inc., 1953, pp. 131-141.

*Murray, Josephine and Bathurst, Effie, *Creative Ways for Children's Programs*. New York: Silver Burdett Co., 1938.

Mursell, James L., *Education for Musical Growth*. Boston: Ginn & Co., 1948, pp. 53-55, 201-209, 169-170, 271-272, 277-281.

Mursell, James L., *Music and the Classroom Teacher*. New York: Silver Burdett Co. 1951, Ch. VIII.

*out of print

Music and abstract art

CHAPTER **VII**

Let's Live with Music

(Music in the Whole School)

Organization of the Music Department

The head of the music department in a city school system is generally known as the *Director of Music*. He employs the music supervisors or consultants and special teachers, and is responsible for the educational philosophy and the coordination of the music throughout the system, from the primary through the secondary schools or junior college.

¶ THE SUPERVISOR — The supervisor is responsible for the music teaching in a certain area. There are vocal supervisors and instrumental supervisors for elementary and secondary schools. A supervisor observes the work of others and gives suggestions for improvement. She sets up workshops and gives in-service training for the general classroom teachers, and coordinates the work in her area. Supervisors set up schedules for visiting. Some announce their visits, and some do not. Counties and states as well as cities have supervisors.

The tendency today is toward consultants rather than supervisors. A true *consultant* goes to a classroom only when invited by the teacher. She acts as a resource person, and keeps her teachers up-to-date on methods and materials. She may give demonstrations and in-service training. She does not observe a teacher in action unless requested to do so.

¶ THE SPECIAL MUSIC TEACHER — At one time the special music teacher had an education limited to a rigid training in music and

[175]

often knew little about children. The special teacher of today has a fairly general education plus a major in music. She teaches only music and may teach it in several schools. She comes into each classroom once or twice weekly for a period of fifteen or twenty minutes of general music. In addition she may have special choruses, instrumental classes, an orchestra or a band, and perhaps some small ensembles. She should be able to play the piano well.

The special teacher, in some schools, works closely with the classroom teacher, *correlating* the music with the other subjects. That is, if a class is studying Mexico, she teaches Mexican music during the music period. Often she acts as consultant for the classroom teacher, who observes her teaching, then carries on the music classes between the special teacher's visits.

¶ THE CLASSROOM TEACHER — The general classroom teacher of today is expected to carry on some musical activities. A special teacher may correlate, but only the classroom teacher can *integrate* music with the other subjects. The classroom teacher can also introduce music for relaxation and recreation at strategic moments during the day.

Music is coming into its own as therapy, but many teachers have not tapped this resource in the classroom. Suppose a class comes into the room after an exciting ball game. How much better for the teacher to give the children a chance to let off steam in a rollicking song or two, followed by more quiet songs, than to order them to be quiet and get to work! Used properly, music can be a great help in discipline as well as morale. A gay humorous song may relieve tensions. A hymn or soft music may be exactly what is needed at times. The resourceful teacher will capitalize upon music throughout the day. When she is at a loss for words, she will let *music* speak.

The classroom teacher with a musical background may be able to teach her own class better than a special teacher, because she is with the children all day, and because she knows them better than someone who sees them for only a short period, occasionally. The teacher with even a very limited musical background may give her class many meaningful musical experiences.

A beginning teacher should not hesitate to call on the supervisor or consultant for help or materials. Asking for help does not mean that a teacher is incapable, but rather indicates a desire to grow. No teacher can be expected to know the philosophy, or all the resources available in a new system. Most schools provide guides, bulletins or handbooks. A new teacher should read these as soon as possible, then call the consultant for any further information desired.

Integration

Music may contribute to the integrated program in varying degrees. The classroom teacher should be aware of the values and the limitations of integration.

For example, the unit on transportation has many possibilities for creative rhythms of the airplane, trucks, buses, trains, and boats of all kinds, but there is a dearth of good songs. If the song is merely *about* a train and gives no feeling of movement, a poem may serve better. *Little Red Caboose* and *The People on the Bus* are good songs and do give a feeling of movement. Sea chanteys are excellent.

There are a number of good recordings for listening, including *Little Train of Caipura* by Villa-Lobos, "Departure" from *Winter Holiday Suite* by Prokofiev, "On the Trail" from *Grand Canyon Suite* by Ferde Grofé, and *Pacific 231* by Honegger. These give the feeling of transportation.

¶ INDIAN MUSIC — Suppose a class is studying about Indians. They may learn a few Indian songs. (See p. 199.) The class should learn that Indians used music in everything they did, that in many tribes each brave had his own theme song which would not be sung by another unless bought from the originator (a forerunner of ASCAP!). They should know that the Indians used drums, rattles, whistles and moraches (notched sticks pressed against inverted gourds for resonance and scraped with straight sticks.) The flute was the courting instrument of some Indian tribes. Children should observe some of the characteristics of Indian music to learn what there is about Indian music that tells us that it *is* Indian. Some of these characteristics include the five-tone scale (pentatonic, similar to the black keys on our piano), much repetition, the downward progression, the use of nonsense syllables, and the lack of harmony. Some Indian music has a regular steady beat and some does not. The drum may play a rhythm entirely different from that of the voice it is supposed to accompany. Indians sing with their mouths almost closed and use a forced tone with a pronounced tremolo. These things may be learned from reading and from listening to authentic recordings. (See p. 199.) The class may enjoy creating a song with Indian characteristics. Young children may make and decorate drums of oatmeal boxes and ice-cream cartons. Most third graders are not strong enough to make good drums using down-ticking or skin heads. However, they can locate nail kegs, barrels and other materials. The teacher can stretch the heads, and the students can paint the drums with nitrate dope and decorate them. Children can bring jacaranda pods, eucalyptus pods, gourds, feathers and bottle tops for making anklets and shakers.

Children may create Indian rhythms for hunting, sowing, threshing, worship and other rituals.

There is little symphonic material for listening which uses Indian themes. (See p. 199.) This lack of good American music which can be traced to the Indians may mean that our composers have not utilized Indian themes as much as they might have done. It may also indicate that some teachers are overemphasizing Indian music. However, Edward MacDowell used Indian themes in his *Indian Suite;* and RCA Victor has an Indian Album in their Basic Record Library for Elementary Schools.

Indians

¶ HAWAIIAN MUSIC — Hawaii is studied in many schools. Most of the Hawaiian songs we know are European with a ukelele accompaniment. The Hawaiians accepted the guitar from visiting sailors and developed from it their own guitars and the ukelele. The *hula* is a song that tells a story. Hawaiians interpret these songs with their hands. For example, rain is interpreted by bringing the fingers fluttering down in imitation of falling raindrops. Native Hawaiians sway the hips while the hands keep a continuous rhythmic motion, going from one interpretation to another.

Elementary school children can learn to play ukeleles, and the hula is a natural form of creative dance. Children like to make their own motions. An Hawaiian ends his hula by bowing, with the hands placed one over the other low in front of the body.

Other rhythmic effects which elementary children enjoy include the use of the *puili stick*. (See p. 169.) Players sit cross-legged or on their knees on the ground or floor, grasp the tube end of the puili stick with the right hand and tap the slit end on the other hand (palm), the ground, the knee, the shoulder, the back of the hand, or the stick of another player in rhythm. Examples:

4 palm, ground, shoulder, back of hand
4 1   2   3   4

4 ground, partner, shoulder, palm
4 1   2   3   4

Children like to create their own rhythmic patterns with the stick. Hawaiians also use feathered gourds (see p. 163) and click flat rocks, *ili-ili*, in their hands similar to the way the Spanish use castanets. Hawaiians sing with a soft, sweet, relaxed tone.

There is very little listening material from Hawaii available at present. Their music is more suitable for the beach than for the concert hall.

¶ MEXICAN MUSIC — On the other hand, the Negroes and the Latin Americans have contributed to our music. The unit on Mexico would be lacking indeed if it did not include a great deal of music. Most of the Mexican people sing and play. The native Indians of Mexico had some interesting instruments including drums, the notched bone with a gourd resonator, and a stringed instrument. The Spaniards brought their music and instruments, including castanets, guitars and violins, to this continent. The Mexican music of today is a fusion of the two. Children usually study about Mexico in about the fifth or sixth grade. They can make maracas, guiros, claves, cabacas and drums, and use them with their Mexican songs and dances. There are many rhythms they may create including those of the making of tortillas and pottery, fiestas, Los Posadas, and bull fights. They may do the traditional Mexican folk-dances, or they may create some with the Mexican flavor. The created dances generally mean more to children. A child who plays the guitar should certainly be urged to bring it to school. One far-sighted principal solved the problem of noise in the halls in the mornings by encouraging a boy to sing and play his guitar. The other children never tired of listening to him and joining him on the songs they knew.

Music in the culmination
of a social studies unit on Mexico

Children may listen to recordings (see p. 200) and observe the characteristics of Mexican music and note their contribution to our own music. They may wish to compose songs with these characteristics. Mexicans have full resonant voices and many of their songs are easily harmonized in thirds and sixths. Spanish and Mexican rhythms are prominent in our modern dance tunes.

¶ NEGRO MUSIC — The music of the Negro may be traced from early African days to the present time. Negro spirituals and work songs are beautiful and rhythmic. The "Pattin' Juba," a combination of patting the foot on the accents and clapping the hands on the off-beats of songs, is enjoyed by children. Children should know about Negro artists such as Marian Anderson, Dorothy Maynor, Roland Hayes and William Warfield. They should hear recordings of Lead-belly singing the blues and Negro folk songs. They should hear the lovely voice of Charity Bailey singing folk songs. Recordings of the De Paur Infantry Chorus are excellent. Some songs from *Showboat* and *Porgy and Bess* will appeal. People of all cultures and races are entitled to their correct names. Songs which violate this principle should not be sung. The correct name for Negroes is "Negroes" or "Colored People."

Negroes have full resonant voices and love to sing at work and at play. They sing when they are happy, and they sing when they are sad or lonely. The story of jazz stems from the Negro. Famous Negro exponents of jazz include Cab Calloway, Duke Ellington and Louis (Satchmo) Armstrong. Our dance tunes of today are descendants of Negro music with its syncopation, and many of them are also influenced by Latin-American rhythms. (See p. 179.)

¶ THE WESTWARD MOVEMENT — Most schools teach the Westward Movement. This unit includes many folk songs and rhythms. The music of the cowboy has influenced American music. The cowboy sang soothing music to quiet the cattle. He used the guitar because it was easy to carry on horseback. At night around the campfire he made his own songs about his horse, his cattle, his "gal" and his life. Some songs reflected his loneliness; others were exciting ballads of outlaws and cattle-branding. Those about the chuck-wagon and "sourdough" were in the humorus vein. Contemporary composers have made good use of cowboy tunes in symphonic literature. (See pp. 129 and 201, 202.)

Creative rhythms may include those of herding cattle into the corral, branding cattle and riding the range. Songs created in connection with units should show understanding of the music as well as the customs of the people.

¶ MUSIC AND SCIENCE — Although music has a great deal to contribute to the science program, many teachers fail to use it. The study of the science of sound may be started in the kindergarten and continued through college. Children may observe how a few grains of sand dance on the head of a drum when it is beaten. This shows that sound is vibration. Children usually enjoy listening to many different kinds of sounds (see p. 10). They should experiment with drums and other rhythm instruments. They learn that the length of the tube, the string, a bar, or a column of air affects the pitch — the longer the tube, the lower the tone. Strings on the autoharp, the harmolin, the piano, and other instruments give high and low pitches depending on the length of the string. The longer

The science of sound

*The
science
of
sound*

bars on the melody bells give the lower tones. Covering the holes on the tonette, the song flute and other wind instruments lengthens the tube and lowers the pitch. Adding and subtracting water from water glasses raises or lowers the pitch. The thickness of strings, metal, or wood affects pitch. Humidity affects drum heads and the pitch of clay flowerpots. Singers tend to flat on humid days. In making chimes, the holes in the tubing should be drilled *before* testing for pitch. Paint affects the tone of metal or wood. Heating a steel rod to make a triangle destroys its tone quality, but it may be restored by heating each side of the triangle afterward. Scraping a notched stick over an inverted gourd gives more resonance than if the gourd is not used. Real orchestral and band instruments may be examined for pitch and tone quality. The film, *Science in the Orchestra,* is one of the best films for classroom use.

¶ MUSIC AND ART — Music can contribute to the art experiences, and vice versa. Children may listen to music, then paint the mood or the picture it suggests to them. They may paint the story the composer had in mind. They may interpret the rhythmic flow of the music with finger-paints, crayons, or poster paint. They may interpret the accents in the music by finger-painting or in design (1:41):

They may interpret the note values in designs (1:21):

Peter and the Wolf by Prokofiev, *Till Eulenspiegel's Merry Pranks* by Richard Strauss, and other descriptive music make fine subjects for murals. Operas such as *Hansel and Gretel* by Humperdinck and *The Mikado* by Gilbert and Sullivan also make good murals. Music

of other lands inspires art work. Abstractions with musical backgrounds are interesting. One teacher asked her eighth grade class°
to fold large pieces of paper in fourths. Then each student made
colored abstractions of the four movements of a Shostakovich Symphony in the four squares of the papers. The results were extremely
interesting.

¶ A "CONCERT" PROJECT — A class°° in Sacramento, California
asked to have a concert using the Standard School Broadcast°°°.
Committees planned programs, stage setting, box office, tickets and
money. Ticket sellers, ushers, stage crew, and doormen were chosen.
Correlation with all subjects developed. Posters and programs
involved art. The class learned about the instruments to be played.
They studied recordings of the selections to be played in order that
they might make their hand-written programs. The children prepared oral and written invitations, acceptances, and "thank you"
notes. Arithmetic was used in "making" money, making change and
handling dollars and cents.

To promote the carry-over of listening into the home, good musical programs heard during week ends or in the early evening hours
were discussed. A record was kept of children who heard the following: Voice of Firestone, Railroad Hour, The Standard Hour,
The Telephone Hour, NBC Symphony, and the New York Philharmonic Symphony. As time went on, the percentage of listeners increased from 25% to 75%. Parents reported their pleasure in the
increased interest in listening to good programs at home.

On the day of the concert, seats in the "Concert Hall" (the
classroom) were arranged in rows facing the "stage" (radio on a
table). For the "backdrop" of the "stage," the class had made a
mural of a conductor directing a symphony orchestra. There was
an orange-crate "box office" near the door. Children called for and
escorted their guests to the box office where they bought tickets,
after which they received programs and were ushered to their seats.

The stage director flicked the lights to signal the program was
about to begin. A hush fell over the audience, and the concert began. The audience listened attentively, occasionally referring to

° Jefferson School, Spokane, Washington, Mary Bramhall, teacher.
°° Grades 3 and 4, Marshall Elementary School.
°°° Latham, Gladys and Mikelson, Geraldine, "Let's Go to the Concert!",
Journal of AERT, Vol. 13, May, 1954, pp. 14-15.

Preparing for "The Concert"

"The Concert"

their programs. At the conclusion of the program the children applauded and filed out of the Concert Hall in groups of twos and threes.

When class work was resumed, an evaluation was made — conduct, interest, good points, likes and dislikes of the music, and ways to improve the next concert.

Integration of music with other subjects is necessary and desirable, but the teacher must be aware of the music that will be missed if only that is used which contributes to units in social studies, science, art, or other subjects. There are many lovely folk and art songs which everyone should know and enjoy, but which cannot be tied to a unit. Most of the truly great listening music can be a part of no unit. These aesthetic and spiritual values may be brought to the children when needed during the day, or during a special period set aside for general music.

General Music

The general music period should take care of the musical experiences which would otherwise be missed. In this period the children should learn many of the fine folk songs that have been recorded by Susan Reed, Burl Ives, Marais and Miranda, Richard Dyer Bennett, Charity Bailey, Jean Ritchie, Tom Glaser, Carl Sandburg, Sam Hinton, Leadbelly, and others. They should learn some of the lovely art songs of our great composers. They should hear great orchestras and artists performing the music they will hear all their lives.

There can and should be no set routine for the general music period. Although there should be variety from day to day, the period is seldom long enough to include singing, rhythmic activities, listening, creative activities, and the use of instruments. The teacher or the teacher and the pupils must select one or two activities, decide what they want to accomplish, and proceed. It is a good plan to take a few minutes at the end of the period for the class to summarize what has been accomplished and what further work is needed in the same activity. In this way continuity is established, and part of the planning for the next day takes place.

Children like to begin the music period with a familiar song or two before proceeding to the new activity. Beginning the period with a successful experience sets the tone of the period. Children also like to learn something new. It may be a new song, or working out the autoharp accompaniment to a familiar song. It may be writing a score for the use of instruments, listening to a record or a performer, or some other activity. There is generally time for only one of these activities. Children like to work hard if they feel the need for learning and if the results are worth the effort. There may be time for polishing something started the day before. It is advisable to end each period with a *successful* experience if at all possible. If it is impossible to complete the activity in progress, it may be well to stop in time to sing a familiar song. The other activity can be resumed on the following day.

Teaching Aids

Each kindergarten room should have a piano, melody bells and a set of rhythm instruments. Other classrooms should have their own melody bells, autoharp, rhythm instruments, and access to a piano. The piano should be *kept in tune*. The tone quality should be pleasing. The low studio type of piano allows the teacher better eye-span. If a large piano is to be shared by several rooms, it should be mounted on wheels.

Every classroom should have a good *three-speed* phonograph. If this is impossible, not more than two or three rooms should be expected to use the same portable phonograph. A poor machine can do more harm than good. Students who operate the phonograph should be instructed how to do so smoothly. If a listening lesson is in progress, the machine should be kept running and the needle merely lifted when necessary. In this way, the motor is kept warm and the sound is good. Records should be held with the edges against the palms of the hands. This prevents the natural oils of the fingers from clogging the grooves. Records should be of the unbreakable type if possible and stored in upright cabinets, away from dust and heat. Heat warps records.

Most schools have film projectors. There are some excellent films; however, the teacher should preview all films and make certain that they are suitable for the class. The operator (student or teacher) should be thoroughly familiar with the machine before showing films to the class. Many schools have special rooms for showing films. (See p. 146 for film sources.)

The *radio* has become an important part of American living. In many homes the radio is going from morning until night. *Tele-*

vision is fast surpassing the status of the radio. The expense seems not to be prohibitive in areas where reception is good. Most schools have radios, and eventually they will have television. If the schools can help children to discriminate in selecting programs, they have served a genuine purpose.

Each geographical area has its own programs in addition to the national networks. The Standard School Broadcast is popular in the West, and FM School of the Air in the East. Most universities, some state education departments, and many large city schools have their own educational programs. Teachers should watch the local newspapers and contact stations for teachers' manuals and broadcast notes. Some of the latter may be obtained by writing to:

American Broadcasting Company, Radio City, New York
Columbia Broadcasting System, 485 Madison Ave., New York
Mutual Broadcasting System, 1440 Broadway, New York
National Broadcasting Company, Radio City, New York
Standard School Broadcasts, 225 Bush St., San Francisco, Cal.

Radio and television may be used in connection with listening lessons. One teacher asked the students to report all music they had heard, both in and out of school. For example, one Monday morning nine students reported hearing *Finlandia* on a Sunday evening broadcast. The class had listened to it a few days before the broadcast. The more music can be a part of daily living, the better.

Opaque projectors are useful in showing small pictures to the class. A picture may be enlarged in a combination slide and opaque projector.

Equipment carts are convenient, not only for the special teacher who must move from room to room, but for teachers who must share. Teachers are more likely to use equipment that is easily accessible. Carts may be purchased, or they may be made in the school shop.

Each room should have some *bulletin board* space especially for music. Pictures of children singing or enjoying other musical activities may be used in the lower grades. Programs, newspaper and magazine clippings, and pictures about music, musicians, composers, or current events are interesting to upper grade children. Pupils like to be responsible for bulletin boards. Sometimes, cartoons about music are in order.

Flannel boards, both with and without the musical staff, are important. Music symbols may be purchased for them. Rolls of flannel of various colors should be available for picture cut-outs.

Special Groups

This book has thus far been concerned with *all* the children in the elementary school. However, the child talented in performance should not be neglected. Some experiences should be provided for those who have the desire and the ability to carry on more advanced activities. There are some who will want to learn to read music well and to perform it. They will be happy to practice additional hours for this experience. Some may want to learn to play orchestral and band instruments, some the piano, and many will want to sing in the school chorus.

¶ THE SCHOOL CHORUS — The size of the chorus will depend upon the size of the school; the interest of the students, the parents, the administrators, and the other teachers; and the number the special teacher wants in the group. In some schools, tryouts are held and only those with beautiful voices and a certain amount of reading ability are accepted. In other schools, any child who is interested may enroll. Some directors start with a small group of good workers and gradually add deserving students, thus avoiding problems of discipline. Others can handle and prefer large groups from the start. Some use only treble voices. Others include the changing voices.

In some schools, choirs are started in the *primary* grades. These children sing in unison with an occasional easy descant. Sound effects with simple instruments enrich their songs. Young children have a very short attention span, so rehearsals should be brief, enjoyable and satisfying. These choirs generally meet once a week. Primary choirs present a grave danger. Children who are not selected often develop emotional blocks which greatly retard or prevent musical development throughout their lives.

All-school choirs usually accept students from grades 4 through 6 or 8. These children should sing some unison songs, some two-part, some three-part, and perhaps some four-part songs, depending upon the types of voices and the ability to carry parts. There is a wealth of good material for elementary choirs. School texts not used currently in the general classroom, collections written for children, and octavo music for children are available. Many special teachers make their own arrangements of folk songs and uncopyrighted material to fit their groups. Either special teachers or teachers with experience in singing in choirs and with some knowledge of conducting should direct these groups.

¶ SMALL ENSEMBLES — Some of the more talented children enjoy singing in harmony in small groups with two or three on a part. Many such groups make their own arrangements, one part singing the melody, another a third or a sixth higher or lower, and a third part using the roots of the chords as a basis for the harmony. Groups of this type should not be drilled and exploited, but should be encouraged to sing musically and in tune.

¶ INSTRUMENTAL CLASSES — Instrumental classes should, of course, be taught by a special teacher or someone with a knowledge of instrumental techniques. Some teachers prefer the homogeneous grouping (like instruments together), while others prefer heterogeneous grouping. Beginning strings play in sharp keys more easily, and beginning wind players find the flat keys easier. For this reason, as well as because of differences in the techniques of tone production, there is generally less mortality in the homogeneous grouping. However, some schools find this grouping impracticable, and some teachers claim that heterogeneous grouping provides a better exploratory situation for the children. String players learn a little about wind instruments, and wind players learn a little about strings. Piano classes should be homogeneous. One or two pianos and a set of keyboards are essential. (Making these keyboards is a good project in industrial arts.)

¶ ORCHESTRAS — In schools in which a number of children can play instruments fairly well, an opportunity should be provided for playing in an orchestra. The instrumentation is seldom balanced in an elementary school, because unusual instruments are neither available nor easy for young beginners to play. Care should be taken that the music selected has parts interesting to all players. Most school arrangements today provide Solo Violin (using positions), Violin A (melody in 1st position), Violin B (a second part that is melodious rather than a series of after-beats), and Violin C (a melodious lower part substituting for the viola which is not ordinarily found in elementary schools. Some teachers restring violins for violas.) Young brass and percussion players do not enjoy long periods of rests. Cross-cues may keep them busy and interested. Because the stringed instruments are more difficult to play, the music for elementary groups should be arranged in keys that are easy for the strings.

¶ BANDS — The more experienced wind and percussion players may be combined into a band. Large schools with many players, and small schools with few string players may have bands. Often the elementary school has a combination orchestra-band. This gives more children a chance to participate.

¶ REHEARSALS — Rehearsals may be scheduled at regular times during school, before school, or after school. Some schools stagger the special group rehearsals so that children will not miss the same activity each time. This plan is not very satisfactory. Children are inclined to forget when to come, and teachers of today do not teach the same subject at the same hour every day. No child should be forced into an organization, but, if he joins, he should attend faithfully.

Programs

Programs may be an outgrowth of classroom music or planned special events. They may be simple or complex. The members of a class may invite their parents to see and hear what they can do in music and the creative arts. One room may give a program culminating a unit and invite the parents, another room, or the whole school to attend. A class may give a creative rhythm or sing songs for another class. Talent shows may be held periodically in the different rooms, and representatives may be selected for an all-school show. Assembly sings should be held from time to time. These may be varied by having different rooms featured in special songs or activities. Songs should be selected and prepared in advance if the assembly sing is to be successful. Primary children who cannot learn all the songs should know some of the choruses so that they can sing with the older children part of the time. Song slides may be used occasionally.

Any program is more interesting if there is variety in the selections. Some lively songs, some serious songs, some nonsense songs, some familiar songs, some new songs, some action songs, some art songs, and some folk songs may be used. One or two instrumental numbers give variety to a vocal program, and, likewise, one or two vocal numbers add interest to an instrumental program. Dances and skits, also, should be considered.

The school choruses and instrumental groups should have opportunities to perform for their schoolmates. These occasions may

An "arm-movement African dance" —
a religious dance — done by seventh grade girls

be learning situations as well as entertainment. One special teacher[*] has individual members of the orchestra stand, play a few bars, and tell a little about their instruments. This is a very meaningful lesson in appreciation.

Some schools emphasize the holy aspect of the Christmas season and give very elaborate programs. Others incorporate the Hanukkah festivities. This is a good lesson in fellowship. Still others feature the customs of various countries or give creative dramatizations of Christmas stories with integrated music.

The best programs are the result of planning by students with the help of teachers. Preparation is the result of research and regular classwork. An excellent program was given as the culmination of studies in the various classes of an elementary school.[**] The

[*] The Clifton Junior High School, Monrovia, California, Miss Geraldine Crawford, teacher.

[**] The Laboratory School, University of Oklahoma, Norman, Oklahoma, Miss Ruth Elder, principal.

theme selected was the history of the state. The primary classes interpreted, through bodily rhythms, the animals in the forests of long ago. The intermediate group interpreted Indian life through rhythms, instruments, and songs. The upper grades were the pioneers in the Westward Movement. They were gathered around a campfire, talking over their old homes and the trek westward, and entertaining themselves with song and dance. These children had done some research, some thinking, and had used discrimination and creativity in planning and producing a cooperative program, which was much more meaningful to them than the production of a printed operetta would have been.

All-City Organizations

All-city organizations may be temporary, organized for some specific program or occasion, or they may be permanent for the year. Members of choruses are chosen for their outstanding performance ability, ability to read, and for balance of parts. Some schools have girls' choruses and treble boys' choruses which sing unison, two-part, or three-part music. There may be boys' choruses for soprano, alto, alto-tenor and bass, or there may be mixed choruses with these parts. Octavo music may be used, or numbers chosen from the fine collections available for these groups. Some directors make their own arrangements of standard songs or folk songs, but they should be careful not to arrange a copyrighted song without permission from the publisher.

Members of orchestras and bands are selected for their performing and reading abilities, and to make a balanced instrumentation. All-city organizations sing and play more advanced music than that used in the individual schools.

¶ REHEARSALS — Rehearsals for these groups run from one and one-half to two hours in length and are scheduled after school or on Saturdays. Most all-city organizations have sectional rehearsals directed by special teachers, and then the sections come together for a full rehearsal under a special teacher or a supervisor. Most of the members are upper grade students who really want to work.

¶ FINANCING CONTINUED ALL-CITY ORGANIZATIONS — In some school systems, financing is handled entirely by the administrations. In other schools, a membership fee is charged to each participant.

Some administrators feel that this investment on the part of the student fosters respect for the organization and appreciation of the opportunity to participate. They feel that both students and parents will then take their responsibilities more seriously. The money is used to purchase music and to pay the instructors.

If a registration fee is required, some provision should be made for the talented child who cannot pay. Scholarships may be awarded, or children may be given opportunities to earn their fees. Fees should be kept low, because there will undoubtedly be some children who will not admit that they cannot afford to enroll. These children may be the very ones who most need the experience.

¶ CONCERTS — All-city groups usually give one or two concerts yearly. Admission may be free or by invitation. Some schools charge admission and use the money to help finance the program. Each group may give its own concert, or groups may combine. If the choral groups and the instrumental groups give separate concerts, variety should be introduced in some manner. Dancing, dramatics, or a different type of music may vary the program. Lighting and simple stage effects help. Concerts should not be too long. Entrances and exits should be well-planned and rehearsed. Quiet games, story-telling, or films should be provided for groups awaiting their turns to perform. If it is impracticable for groups to hear each other at the concert, certainly provision should be made for them to do so at the dress rehearsal.

¶ UNIFORMS OR DRESS — Uniforms are not necessary. White shirts or blouses and dark trousers or skirts are effective. Dresses and shirts in pastel shades are also suitable. Miscellaneous colors scattered in large groups give a pleasing effect.

In a school where the band members wear flashy uniforms, certainly the members of the orchestra should have something comparable in the way of dress. The music and the comradeship, not the uniform, however, should be the incentive.

¶ MOTHERS' ORGANIZATIONS — Band and orchestra mothers have been known both to help and to hinder school organizations. Sometimes strong parental groups will help with organization, promotion, and financing. They may get behind the schools and the instructors and push the organizations. Some such groups have been known to raise funds for providing instruments and scholarships for underprivileged children, and for purchasing unusual and expensive instruments such as 'cellos, double basses, tubas, oboes, and timpani.

On the other hand, such a group has been known to wreck an organization by petty jealousies, bickering, and a tendency to dictate to the school. Before starting such an organization, it is important to hold conferences of representatives, teachers, and administrators to discuss the problems frankly. A constitution should be drawn up and approved by all concerned.

¶ EVALUATION OF ALL-CITY ORGANIZATIONS — Personnel must be selected fairly and tactfully. Otherwise, some children who are not selected will be disappointed unnecessarily. Organizations which are student-governed contribute considerably to the growth of their members. Each group should elect its officers and these officers should be allowed to function. They can take roll, distribute and collect music, collect fees, set up rehearsal rooms, and save the teachers many time-consuming duties. The students have the thrill of working in large organizations which are able to produce artistic results. They learn to know children outside their own schools and neighborhoods. They learn to assume responsibilities, and to work with others. It is good for a child who is outstanding in his own school to work with others just as talented as he is, and to experience the unique thrill of excellent performance in large groups.

It is important that talented children who take part in special groups do not acquire a feeling of superiority. They should not be excused from participation in music in the general classroom. Rather, they should bring help and inspiration and a desire to contribute to the success of general music.

Evaluation of the School Music Program and Teaching

Evaluation necessarily depends upon the objectives. These should be established by everyone concerned. The students, the parents and the community, the special teachers, the classroom teachers, the consultants, and the administrators should all be considered. The setting up of objectives in each individual school seems time-consuming, but it can be done, and it can be a rewarding experience for all.

Every teacher should stop occasionally and ask himself if he is accomplishing what he set out to accomplish. If not, why? Such questions as the following may serve as guides in the self-evaluation of a teacher:

Do I, the teacher,
1. Promote continuous development in my pupils?
2. Provide a variety of musical activities?
3. Encourage originality?
4. Attend concerts, listen to records, radio and TV programs, and keep up with current musical events, significant both nationally and locally?
5. Take advantage of every opportunity to grow, musically, by participating in choirs and instrumental groups?
6. Take advantage of in-service training such as workshops and institutes?
7. Take advantage of available college courses in music?
8. Make the most of available consultant service?
9. Attend Music Educators' Conferences?

Do my pupils
1. Really enjoy singing?
   (Facial expressions of the singers are good indicators.)
2. Comment if music is occasionally omitted from the program?
3. Bring records, books, pictures, and clippings about music to school?
4. Talk about radio, TV, cinema music, and programs they have heard?
5. Participate in outside musical activities, such as assembly sings, chorus, orchestra, and instrumental classes?
6. Ask to hear repeat performances of records played in class?
7. Use the listening booth?
8. All contribute in some way to the musical activities of the class?
9. Read library books about music?

Other tangible evidences of the success or failure of music in the schools can be accumulated through the use of such techniques as:
1. Hobby questionnaires.
   Do children check musical activities?
2. Preference questionnaires showing types of records, songs, or programs children prefer.
3. Informal chats with recreational leaders of the community.

4. Informal chats with parents.
5. Informal chats with private music teachers of the community. Sometimes these teachers offer scholarships to deserving underprivileged children.
6. Chats with pupils.

A good music program in the schools requires the interest and the cooperation of everyone concerned — children, classroom teachers, special teachers, administrators, and the community. Each has something to contribute. The value of music lies in what it can do for the child.

General Assignments

1. In the light of what you have learned about children and music, revise your objectives for music in the elementary school. (See Chapter I.)
2. Make a check list of activities which you intend to introduce to the children in your music classes. This list may be used from time to time during your teaching career to help you maintain a well-rounded program.
3. Construct a self-evaluation chart which you can use to advantage when you are teaching.
4. Describe some elementary school music programs you have seen. Evaluate them in terms of their effect on the children, the teachers, and the spectators.
5. Describe the type of administrative organization in the music department of your local schools.
6. List the teaching aids you would like if you were teaching elementary music. List them in the order of their importance.
7. Plan the musical aspects of a specific classroom unit. Give specific:
> Songs and sources (use bibliographical order)
> Creative rhythmic activities
> Other creative activities (musical)
> Records for listening (title, composer, company)
> Suggested use of instruments
8. Re-read the Preface to this book.

A music center

Some Suggested Sources of Music Materials for Representative Units

INDIAN

Songs

Armitage, Theresa et al, *Our First Music*. Boston: C. C. Birchard & Co., 1941.

Armitage, Theresa et al, *Merry Music*. Boston: C. C. Birchard & Co., 1939, 1953.

Beattie, John W. et al, *American Singer*, Bk. 2. New York: American Book Co., 1954.

Densmore, Frances, *Indian Action Songs*. Boston: C. C. Birchard & Co., 1921.

Gale, Albert and the Krones, *Songs and Stories of the American Indians*. Chicago: Neil A. Kjos Music Co., 1949.

Hoffman, Charles, *War Whoops and Medicine Songs*. Boston: Boston Music Co., 1952.

McConathy, Osbourne et al, *New Music Horizons*. Bks. 4, 5. New York: Silver Burdett Co., 1944.

Pitts, Lilla Belle et al, *Singing and Rhyming*. Boston: Ginn & Co., 1950.

Records

American Indians of the Southwest (Folkways), Taos, Hopi, Apache and Pueblo.

Authentic American Indian Songs and Chants. Canyon Records 134-163.

Hopi Butterfly, Eagle, Buffalo and Victory Dances

Apache Mountain Spirit and Sunrise Dances; Lightning Song

Navajo War, Sun, Gift, Shield and Hoop Dances

Navajo Grinding, Love, Riding, Goat, Happy Songs

Jemez Cradle Buffalo, Hunting and Harvest Dances

Omaha War, Dance, Flag and Contest Dance Songs

Kiowa War Dance

Taos Horse Tail, War, Social Dances

Zuni, Buffalo, Planting, and Squaw Dances

Comanche Song

Flathead Indian Music (recorded in Montana), Folkways

Indian Album, RCA Basic Record Library for Elementary Schools. (Some authentic, some composed)

MacDowell, Edward, *Indian Suite #2*, Mercury

Natay, Navajo Singer (authentic Hopi, Navajo, Zuni), Canyon

Sioux and Navajo Music, Folkways

Tewa Love Song sung by Pop Chalee, Canyon

Books for the Teacher

Brewster, Benjamin, *The First Book of Indians*. New York: Franklin Watts, Inc., 1950.

Cotton, Marian and Bradburn, Adelaide, *Music throughout the World*. Boston: C. C. Birchard & Co., 1953, pp. 10-12.

Fletcher, Alice, *Indian Games and Dances, with Native Songs*. Boston: C. C. Birchard & Co., 1915.

Mason, Bernard, *Drums, Tom-toms and Rattles*. New York: A. S. Barnes & Co., 1938.

Mason, Bernard, *Dances and Stories of the American Indian*. New York: A. S. Barnes & Co., 1944.

Salomon, Julian, *Book of Indian Crafts and Indian Lore*. New York: Harper & Bros., 1928.

Tooze, Ruth and Krone, Beatrice Perham, *Literature and Music*. Englewood Cliffs, N.J.: Prentice-Hall, Inc., 1955, Ch. XIII.

MEXICAN

Songs

Armitage, Theresa et al, *Music Everywhere*. Boston: C. C. Birchard & Co., 1943, 1955.

Armitage, Theresa et al, *Our Land of Song*. Boston: C. C. Birchard & Co., 1942, 1956

Beattie, John W. et al, *American Singer*, Bk. 5. New York: American Book Co., 1955.

Dykema, Peter W. et al, *Music in the Air*. Boston: C. C. Birchard & Co., 1947.

Dykema, Peter W. et al, *Sing Out!*

Boston: C. C. Birchard & Co., 1946.

Gonzales, F., *La Hora del Canto*. New York: Edward B. Marks Music Corp., 1942.

Krone, Beatrice and Max, *Inter-Americana*. Chicago: Neil A. Kjos Music Co., 1945. (Includes "Los Posados" Christmas Festival)

Krone, Beatrice and Max, *Spanish and Latin-American Songs*. Chicago: Neil A. Kjos Music Co., 1942.

McConathy, Osbourne et al, *New Music Horizons*, Bks. 5, 6. New York: Silver Burdett Co., 1946.

McLaughlin, Roberta and Stanchfield, Bessie, *Cancioncitas*. Minneapolis: Paul A. Schmitt Music Co., 1948.

Millan, Amalia and the Krones, *Mexican Folk Songs*. Chicago: Neil A. Kjos Music Co., 1948.

Munoz, Maria and Pastor, Angela, *Canta Conmigos*. New York: American Book Co., 1946.

Pan American Union, *Latin American Song Book*. Boston: Ginn & Co., 1942.

Pitts, Lilla Belle et al., *Singing in Harmony*. Boston: Ginn & Co., 1951.

Writer's Program, New Mexico, *Spanish-American Song and Game Book*. New York: A. S. Barnes & Co., 1942.

Zanzig, Augustus D., *Singing America*. Boston: C. C. Birchard & Co., 1940.

Records

Indian Music of Mexico, Folkways

Jarabe, Tapito, Cielito Lindo, La Golondrina, Musical Sound Books

Latin-American Folk Songs, Bowmar Records

Little Pedro and the Street Singers (Primary), Children's Record Guild

Mexican Cowboy Songs, sung by Los Rancheros, Decca

Music of Mexico, Decca

Songs of Mexico, Folkways

"Xochipili-Macquilixochitl" from *Program of Mexican Music* by Chavez, Columbia

Books for the Teacher

Cotton, Marian and Bradburn, Adelaide, *Music throughout the World*. Boston: C. C. Birchard & Co., 1953, p. 38.

Nordholm, Harriet and Bakewell, Ruth V., *Keys to Teaching Junior High School Music*. Minneapolis: Paul A.

Schmitt Music Co., 1953, p. 65.

Toor, Frances, *A Treasury of Mexican Folkways*. New York: Crown Publishers, 1947.

Tooze, Ruth and Krone, Beatrice Perham, *Literature and Music*. Englewood Cliffs, N.J.: Prentice-Hall, Inc., 1955, Ch. XVII.

NEGRO

Songs

Dykema, Peter W. et al, *Music in the Air*. Boston: C. C. Birchard & Co., 1947.

Dykema, Peter W. et al, *Sing Out!* Boston: C. C. Birchard & Co., 1946.

Landeck Beatrice, *Git on Board*. New York: Edward B. Marks Music Corp. 1950.

Landeck, Beatrice, *Songs to Grow On*. New York: Edward B. Marks Music Corp., 1950.

McConathy, Osbourne et al, *New Music Horizons*, Bk. 6. New York: Silver Burdett Co., 1946.

Negro Spirituals of all kinds.

Pitts, Lilla Belle et al, *Singing in Harmony*. Boston: Ginn & Co., 1951.

Pitts, Lilla Belle et al., *Singing Together*. Boston: Ginn & Co., 1951.

Seeger, Ruth Crawford, *American Folk Songs for Children*. Garden City, N. Y.: Doubleday & Co., 1949.

Zanzig, Augustus D., *Singing America*. Boston: C. C. Birchard & Co., 1940.

Records

Deep River sung by William Warfield, Columbia

From the Canebrake, by Samuel Gardner.

God's Trombones and other Spirituals, sung by Fred Waring and his Pennsylvanians, Decca.

Jazz Band, Young People's Records.

Juba Dance, Nathaniel Dett

Jungle Drums, Decca

Leadbelly, Vol. 4, Stinson LP 51.

Marian Anderson Sings Spirituals, RCA Victor

"Nigerian Lullaby" from *Follow the Sunset*, sung by Charity Bailey, Folkways

Play Parties, sung by Leadbelly, Stinson

---

*out of print

The Story of Jazz for Children, narrated by Langston Hughes, Folkways
Swing Low, sung by De Paur Infantry Chorus, Columbia
Take This Hammer, sung by Leadbelly, Folkways
Underground Railroad, Young People's Records
Work Songs and Spirituals, sung by De Paur Infantry Chorus, Columbia

Books for Children
Hughes, Langston, *The First Book of Jazz.* New York: Franklin Watts, Inc., 1955.
Hughes, Langston, *The First Book of Negroes.* New York: Franklin Watts, Inc., 1952.

Books for the Teacher
Children's Music Center, *Jazz in Music Education.* Children's Music Center, 2858 West Pico Blvd., Los Angeles, Calif., 1956.
Cotton, Marian and Bradburn, Adelaide, *Music throughout the World.* Boston: C. C. Birchard & Co., 1953, pp. 7-8, 12-14, 24, 38, 166-167, 229.
Hughes, Langston, *Famous Negro Music Makers.* New York: Dodd, Mead & Co., 1955.
Johnson, James Weldon and Johnson, J. Rosamond, *The Books of American Negro Spirituals.* New York: Viking Press, Inc., 1940.
Nordholm, Harriet and Bakewell, Ruth V., *Keys to Teaching Junior High School Music.* Minneapolis: Paul A. Schmitt Music Co., 1953, pp. 70-79.
Pitts, Lilla Belle, *Music Integration in the Junior High School.* Boston: C. C. Birchard & Co., 1935, pp. 114-117.
Tooze, Ruth and Krone, Beatrice Perham, *Literature and Music.* Englewood Cliffs, N.J.: Prentice-Hall, Inc., 1955, Ch. XII.

THE WESTWARD MOVEMENT

Songs
Armitage, Theresa et al, *Our Land of Song.* Boston: C. C. Birchard & Co., 1942, 1956.
Beattie, John W. et al, *American Singer,* Bk. 5. New York: American Book Co., 1955.
Boni, Margaret, *Fireside Book of Fa-*

vorite American Songs. New York: Simon & Schuster, 1952.
Dykema, Peter W. et al, *Music in the Air.* Boston: C. C. Birchard & Co., 1947.
Dykema, Peter W. et al, *Sing Out!* Boston: C. C. Birchard & Co., 1946.
Felton, Harold W., *Cowboy Jamboree.* New York: Alfred A. Knopf, 1951.
Ives, Burl, *The Burl Ives Song Book.* New York: Ballantine Books, 1953.
Landeck, Beatrice, *Songs My True Love Sings.* New York: Edward B. Marks Music Corp., 1946.
Lomax, John A., and Alan, *American Ballads and Folk Songs.* New York: The Macmillan Co., 1934, 1953.
Lomax, John A., and Alan, *Folk Song: U.S.A.* New York: Duell, Sloan and Pearce, 1947.
Sandburg, Carl, *The American Songbag.* New York: Harcourt, Brace & Co., Inc., 1927, 1946.
Sandburg, Carl, *New American Songbag.* New York: Broadcast Music, Inc., 1950.
Scott, Tom, *Folk Songs for Singing.* New York: Charles H. Hansen Music Corp., 1948.
Scott, Tom, *Sing of America.* New York: Thomas Y. Crowell Co., 1947.
Seeger, Ruth C., *American Folksongs for Children.* Garden City, N. Y.: Doubleday & Co., 1948.
Sires, Ina, *Songs of the Open Range.* Boston: C. C. Birchard & Co., 1928.
Wilson, Harry, *Songs of the Hills and Plains.* Chicago: Hall & McCreary Co., 1943.

Records
Billy the Kid, Aaron Copland, Capitol
Chisholm Trail, Young People's Records
Cowboy Ballads, sung by Cisco Huston, Folkways
Death Valley Suite, Ferde Grofé, Capitol
Git Along Little Dogie, sung by Frank Luther, Decca
"Go 'Long, Little Dogies" from *Follow the Sunset,* sung by Charity Bailey, Folkways
Going West, Young People's Records
Grand Canyon Suite, Ferde Grofé, Capitol

Home on the Range, sung by Frank Luther, Decca
Let's Go to the Rodeo, Young People's Records
Prairie, Leo Sowerby
Rodeo, Aaron Copland, Capitol
Wagon Wheels, Morton Gould, Columbia
Western Symphony, Hershey Kay, Vox

See Ch. V for other suggestions.
Books for the Teacher
Botkin, B. O., *A Treasury of Western*

Folklore. New York: Crown Publishers, 1951.
Cotton, Marian and Bradburn, Adelaide, *Music throughout the World.* Boston: C. C. Birchard & Co., 1953, pp. 8-10.
Nordholm, Harriet and Bakewell, Ruth V., *Keys to Teaching Junior High School Music.* Minneapolis: Paul A. Schmitt Music Co., 1953, pp. 16-22.
Pitts, Lilla Belle, *Music Integration in the Junior High School.* Boston: C. C. Birchard & Co., 1935, pp. 119-124.

The Westward Movement

General References

BOOKS

Adams, Fay, *Educating America's Children*. New York: Ronald Press, 1946, pp. 431-432.

Andrews, Frances M. and Leeder, J., *Guiding Experiences in Music in the Junior High School*. New York: Prentice-Hall, Inc., 1953.

Baer, Marian E., *Sound*. New York: Holiday House, 1952.

Bauer, Marion, and Peyser, Ethel, *How Music Grew*. New York: G. P. Putnam's Sons, 1939.

Botkin, B. O., *The Sidewalks of America*. Folklore, Legends, Sagas, Customs, Songs, and Sayings of City Folks. New York: Bobbs-Merrill Co., 1954.

Buchanan, Fannie R., *How Man Made Music*. Chicago: Follett Publishing Co., 1954.

Children's Music Center, *Recommended Records and Books*. 2858 W. Pico Blvd., Los Angeles: Children's Music Center (revised yearly).

Cotton, Marian and Bradburn, Adelaide, *Music throughout the World*. Boston: C. C. Birchard & Co., 1953.

Dykema, Peter W. and Cundiff, Hannah M., *School Music Handbook*. Boston: C. C. Birchard & Co., 1955.

Flagg, Marion, *Musical Learning*. Boston: C. C. Birchard & Co., 1949, pp. 172-185.

Geraldton, James, *The Story of Sound*. New York: Harcourt, Brace & Co., Inc., 1948.

Grant, Parks, *Music for Elementary Teachers*. New York: Appleton-Century-Crofts, Inc., 1951, Ch. XXIV, XXV.

Mathews, Paul W., *You Can Teach Music*. New York: E. P. Dutton & Co., Inc., 1953, pp. 142-156.

McKinney, Howard D., *Music and Man*. New York: American Book Co., 1948.

Morgan, Hazel Nohavec, "Music in American Education," *Music Education Source Book*, No. 2. Washington: MENC, 1955, pp. 63-64.

Mursell, James L., *Education for Musical Growth*. Boston: Ginn & Co., 1948, pp. 148, 273.

Mursell, James L., *Music and the Classroom Teacher*. New York: Silver Burdett Co., 1951, pp. 32, 161.

Music Educators National Conference, *Handbook on 16 mm. Films for Music Education*. 1201 16th St., N.W., Washington 6, D.C.: MENC, 1951.

Myers, Louise Kifer, *Teaching Children Music in the Elementary School*. New York: Prentice-Hall, Inc., 1956, Ch. 10, 11, 12.

Nesbitt, Marion, *A Public School for Tomorrow*. New York: Harper & Bros., 1953, pp. 61-79.

Nordholm, Harriet and Bakewell, Ruth V., *Keys to Teaching Junior High School Music*. Minneapolis: Paul A. Schmitt Music Co., 1953.

Pitts, Lilla Belle, *Music Integration in the Junior High School*. Boston: C. C. Birchard & Co., 1935.

Schneider, Herman and Nina, *Follow the Sunset*. (Lullabies of all lands.) Garden City, N. Y.: Doubleday & Co., 1952.

Tooze, Ruth and Krone, Beatrice, *Literature and Music*. Englewood Cliffs, N.J.: Prentice-Hall, Inc., 1955.

MUSIC MAGAZINES

Educational Music Magazine, Educational Music Bureau, 30 East Adams St., Chicago 3, Ill. 4 times per year.

Film Notes, National Film Music Council, 26 East 83rd St., New York, 28. Five times per year plus some bulletins.

Instrumentalist, The (for school band and orchestra directors and instrumental teachers). The Instrumental Co., 1418 Lake St., Evanston, Ill. Monthly Sept.-May.

Journal of AERT, Ass'n. for Education by

Radio and Television, 228 N. La Salle St., Chicago. Monthly Sept.-May.

Journal of Research in Music Education, Music Educators National Conference, 1201 16th St., N.W., Washington 6, D.C. 2 issues per year.

Keyboard Jr. (for junior and senior high school students). Monthly Sept.-May. In lots of five subscriptions. 1346 Chapel St., New Haven 11, Conn.

Music Educators Journal, Music Educators National Conference, 1201 16th St., N.W., Washington 6, D.C. 6 issues yearly. (Official music educators' magazine.)

Music Journal, Delaware Water Gap, Pa. Monthly.

Musical America, 1401 Steinway Bldg., 113 W. 57th St., New York 19. Monthly.

School Musician (for instrumental students and teachers), 4 East Clinton St., Joliet, Ill. Monthly.

Teaching Tools (radio and television), VerHoesen Publishing Co., 1159 N. Highland Ave., Los Angeles, Calif.

Young Keyboard Jr. (for elementary school students). Monthly Sept.-May. In lots of five subscriptions. 1346 Chapel St., New Haven 11, Conn.

Index

Refer also to the Index in *Let's Make Music*, companion to this book.